The Search for a Usable Future

The
SEARCH
for a
USABLE
FUTURE

by Martin E. Marty

Harper & Row, Publishers
New York, Evanston, and London

FIRST EDITION

LIBRARY OF CONGRESS CATALOG CARD NUMBER: 69-10473

M-S

To Harold E. Fey and Kyle Haselden

Hope is the same thing as remembering

—Paul Ricoeur

Contents

Contents

Foreword

*F*ive years have passed since I
undertook a moratorium on book writing. Two works on history,
growing out of my professorial vocation, have been taking shape
during that time. The present work, however, grows out of an
editorial avocation and includes opinion along with observation,
advice along with analysis. The projects are complementary, re-
flecting my belief that devotion to nineteenth-century history
should not preclude interest in the twentieth century on one hand
and, on the other, that concern for the contemporary profits from
a grounding in history. If the other works will demonstrate that
a church *historian* talks about history, this one suggests that he
may also want to talk about the *Church*. The early chapters are
reflections on the ways an analytical historian relates to the future. The middle chapters discuss the political role of one power
force in society that is contending for a place in the future, the
Church. The final section looks at the life and health of the
Church and thus helps readers see this book in continuity with

The New Shape of American Religion (1959), written near the end of the religious revival, and *Second Chance for American Protestants* (1963), published during the ensuing years of reform and renewal.

While my back was turned, the Church has seen the Vatican Council, the rise and fall of secular-radical-new-death-of-God theology, and vast cultural changes. This is my first book-length comment on these turns. None of these chapters has been previously published.

Some of the material was delivered orally in the Oreon Scott Lectureship at Phillips University, Enid, Oklahoma; the Carver-Barnes Lectures at Southeastern Baptist Theological Seminary, Wake Forest, North Carolina; and the Alumni Lectures at Princeton Theological Seminary. The argument of this book was presented and tested in different, undeveloped form in a number of lectures during the past several years. Audiences at some of these occasions have asked whether what they heard would ever appear in print. I told them it would; here it is. Let me thank Richard Koenig of Amherst, Massachusetts, for encouraging me to write this kind of book "and not just a book reporting on what everyone else has said."

MARTIN E. MARTY

Chicago, Illinois

1

The Sense of a Useless Past

$\mathcal{M}$en act, in large measure, in the light of the futures which they envision or project. But the raw material for their action comes from remembered ideas, words, events, images, and models. Thus their search for usable futures in any era will be grounded in their view of particular pasts. At some times a past will seem easily accessible; at other times, very little in it will speak directly to a later generation: it will seem to be useless for the formation of the future and thus for present action.

When a group of dissenting historians gathered to criticize the prevailing way of looking at American life they named their essays *Towards a New Past.*[1] The old version of the past was not acceptable to them and they had to create out of different historical materials and with differing methods of approach the basis for a new way of perceiving the present and planning for the future. When the American civil rights revolution took on a more militant character, spokesmen for black identity began to demand courses on Afro-American history in the schools. To many this seemed like a curious call, for it came at a time when young white Americans were said to be disinterested in the lessons of history. But the blacks knew that while one past had become useless for them, another might speak.

Henry Steele Commager has told of the ways the citizens of the new American republic had to create a sense of history; he spoke of *The Search for a Usable Past*.[2] These citizens did what people regularly do: they reinterpret or invent a view of what has gone before for their present needs and purposes.

If such action is regular, people may rightfully ask whether history has no power of its own to speak directly; is it only the product of the professional historians, leaders of power movements, or forward-looking citizens? The answer to the question could be: "that depends." At times in history people sense their place in a stream of events; the past speaks clearly and is obviously useful. Men write annals of what goes on in the seat of power. They chronicle day-to-day affairs while assuming their importance.

At other times they feel cut off. The annals seem to be pointless and chronicles gather dust. People turn to visionaries and dreamers or respond to the call to enjoy the moment. The historian in such years quietly keeps his craft alive, waiting for that moment when a society may once again in uncertainty "stop to think."[3] Or in such years they may greet the forward-looking enthusiasms of their day by looking backward with compensatory vigor,[4] as the first great generation of American historians were said to have done.

To speak of the sense of a useless past, then, is not to take a nihilist's view of historical life but rather to point to the creative possibility of the moment. The historian accounts also for that recent past which people call "the present." In the later years of the twentieth century his accounting may cause him to record his contemporaries' widespread sense that a whole tradition has been exhausted, that nothing in Euro-American, Western, Christian, or modern civilization can automatically be assumed to be alive to wide sectors of the society.

The observation that a tradition seems remote or spent can be made even in a time when historical studies go on as never before, when new skills and methods and energies, new bases for storing and retrieving lore of the past, are available.

For some, the past has become useless because the magnetic pull of history draws attention to new sources of power. Thus many speak of the movement from a European to an Asian focus. In aquatic imagery, the center of curiosity after centuries is no longer the Atlantic but is now the Pacific Ocean. The American political tradition is regarded by many no longer to be able to sustain the tensions of a conflict-oriented populace in a tense world. The formal expression of the Western spiritual life for many centuries, the catholic Christian Church, eludes the grasp of living people of faith. No sooner was Vatican Council II disbanded than a generation rose which was not able to accept its struggles or its achievements as addresses to new problems. Theologians, once the custodians of the Christian antique shop, shared in the sense of rejection of the old and seemed intoxicated by the forward-looking spirit.

The young ordinarily best reveal the sense of an exhausted tradition, of a useless past. During the years of dramatic change people came to speak of a gap between the old and the young. The young constituted a generation;[5] that is, they were a body of people who had experienced similar formative experiences in the decisive years of their development. They lived in the same houses and walked the same streets as did their elders, but the world looked different to them. They seemed to have a different kind of consciousness, a new set of sensibilities, a different way of perceiving the world.

External events had much to do with the purported change. Within a ten-year span the Western world, at least, had become aware of terms and concepts which would have been meaningless sooner: automation, cybernetics, Sputnik, the Third World, the mass media revolution—one could run through the whole catalogue of expectables; these were symbolic of profoundly felt changes.

Historians, in order to perform their duties and to be of help to their readers, give symbolic names to complex moments of history. They speak of the Renaissance or the Enlightenment, which are not events in the same way that the bombing of Pearl Harbor or the assassination of President Kennedy was. But in the 1960s many observers including many historians found that they could not easily coin terms which implied change within the tradition. A Renaissance meant a rebirth out of the old; the Enlightenment implied a change in a partly darkened culture. But now, it was argued, the sense of repudiation and rejection was so strong that they could not observe the coming generation picking up the traditional culture for the purpose of transforming it.

The thoughtful and reflective person knows that people cannot and do not start from scratch in history. Sooner or later, after the rejection, they begin to rebuild. Once again, they have to turn to some sort of past for their materials. Those for whom the act of rejecting has become pathological are not able to participate. They remain alienated, they experience frustration or drift, they express resentment or rage.

Signs of the sense of an exhausted tradition were obvious in the decade in question. The university, in an age of mass higher education, came to be a new power center. And the celebrated campus revolts showed that students were not merely interested in adapting an old system; many of them wanted to "bring the system down" because it no longer even potentially could be the bearer of human values. The United Nations was no longer the soapbox of three or four great powers; the old rationale had disappeared, and scores of identity-conscious new nations used it to contend for their space under the sun: world power was appearing in nontraditional ways. Conventional Canada celebrated its centennial with an *Expo* which attracted millions by projecting images and sounds that could not be measured by conventional standards of exhibit and display: op and pop art and psychedelic sounds were appropriated by Great Plains grandmothers.

The clash or gap was not really simply between generations but between epochs. During the Vietnam War it became obvious, for example, that a historic approach to war had become obsolete. Young men, shaped by television, reformist religion, and mass higher education, were not able to fit the military action into previously formed patterns of conscience. They bewildered some of their elders by having to dissent and resist the draft. Other elders concurred with them, arguing that an epochal change had occurred: a new kind of person in a new kind of society seemed to be on the scene. He had "seen" war as his elders had not; the pointless, groundless, body-counting military action had little in common with the old ground-occupying concept of marching men of valor of which the tradition spoke.

These illustrations from centers of learning, of popular culture, of international action, and of war could be extended indefinitely. They share the mood of a moment when epochs change, when "everything is up for grabs." People in such a society learn to tolerate the outrageous for the sake of experiment. The young person who asks what "pacification" could possibly mean, after he had seen the films of pacification in destroyed Vietnamese villages; the one who queried his elders about "reconciliation" after he saw what a century of reconciliation in the patterns of segregation or a called-for integration in American cities meant— such a person was showing how little hope people could place in those "-ation" words which preserve inert ideas of an old culture. They were asking their elders for the acceptance of apparently outrageous alternative approaches; they were called upon to expand and stretch their consciousness and to tolerate the shocking and the new.

The response of many custodians of the old epoch was to see the experiment as mere anarchy. From many of them came a call for return to the old system, in the interest of order over against misused freedom. Those who spoke for sudden change seemed to the preservers to be reckless innovators, tamperers with tradition, potentially violent stormers of the secure citadels. On the other hand, the innovators spoke of their fear lest the new media and the new technology serve to imprison people, to delude them. The media, particularly to the more radical critics, were the tools of commercial barons who trivialized life and bought off discontent.[6]

Those who felt left out of the old system were not exclusively young people. An analysis of power relations in the United States indicates that perhaps half the population felt cut off from the formal embodiment of the old tradition. They were not always in a situation of political power: the system made possible consolidations of power expressive of the old. But in para-political ways like demonstrations, strikes, protests, dissents, and grumbling or creative foot-dragging, the alternative power was finding expression.

The cluster of dissenters left out some groups which earlier would have belonged with them. Thus the American labor movement had come, for the most part, to be part of the conservative power force. Its struggle was over, and it seemed to take little role in understanding the Third World or the racial revolution in America. The political liberals often seemed to cling to views of an imperial West which to the new clusters represented a dying traditional view. It is profitable to see who has been left out of the national consensus, the people for whom a particular past seemed useless at best and dehumanizing at worst.

Such a catalogue would inevitably begin with the militant blacks. They represented the present form of one of America's obsessive issues, one which had been with the society since slaves were brought from Africa early in the seventeenth century. Few Americans could speak seriously of issues for more than a few minutes without having to deal with the presence of new symbolic leaders of twenty million Americans, most of whom were not "cut in" to the past which had been assumed by white America.

Now located in urban centers, where organization was possible as it had not been in the rural dispersion, the American blacks were experiencing a "revolution of rising expectations." The media, especially television, portrayed the range of goods "priced for every pocketbook." (The looters in many cities, the same media were later to point out, were discriminating: they had learned from television just which brands of television to steal during a riot!) Victims of racism, newly conscious of their ties to Africa and the rest of the non-Western world, these leaders were increasingly successful at speaking for millions.

A second cluster, as already implied, lives on the campuses. The students found much of the past and its consensus to be useless. While the apathetic majority remained on the campuses, to the comfort of conservative elders, the leadership had passed to people who rejected the societal lore through militancy or by dropping out.

In the later years of the 1960s it was instructive to observe who served as gurus or shamans for these campus seekers. Who would draw a crowd across the lines of various fields or disciplines? While many of their names are soon forgotten, during their moment they reveal a common sense of the now and the new and a common rejection of a tradition: Norman O. Brown, Marshall McLuhan, Timothy Leary, LeRoi Jones, Buckminster Fuller, Allen Ginsberg, Susan Sontag, Thomas Altizer, Tom Wolfe, all rejected conventional canons of interpreting the past and united to imply that it was voiceless to a generation that needed a voice.

At the side of the students stood the dissenting academy;[7] by this observers mean the faculty members who reject many of the assumptions of the higher learning in America. In their vision, the academy is part of a repressively tolerant system, one which misuses people. It draws young people in the interest of learning but succeeds only in preparing them to adapt to a military and industrial system which will kill them or others, or which at least will deprive them of opportunities to become fully human. The dissenting academy may number only scores of thousands to match the student millions, but its influence on others, at least potentially, is great.

The poor belong in such a list. Where they are rural or non-black they often remain invisible and unorganized. They lack the symbolic leaders such as those that have emerged in the black and academic communities. Often mistrustful of such potential leaders, isolated, and burying their discontent under layers of pride, they are not part of the consensus and share none of the benefits of the system; they represent a potential source of discontent and change. Now and then, as in the case of West Coast grape pickers, some of them find a voice and can organize a movement. Until then, they serve as a base for alienation and, as the city remains a magnet, of the urban malaise.

The New Left is one of the most assertive if not among the better organized of the clusters of people left out of the consensus and the tradition. The New Left, since it often finds its home on campuses, is one of the more literate of the discontented groups. And, being literate, it finds historical writing and reasoning to be accessible. But this does not mean that it finds the immediate past of the society useful for developing its own vision of a humane world. The New Left, of course, is a name for many contending forces. Among them are those who believe that the minority has the right to take history in its own hands; that, even when rejected at the ballots, it may assert itself, perhaps violently, to gain its way, for it alone has insight into what is good for men in society. Others are more conventionally in the radical liberal tradition of free expression. The past often seems useless in pursuit of such a vision. Even Left heroes, like Karl Marx, fit too conventionally into a dying Western tradition and the New Left picks some of its heroes from a less rationally complex and more immediately violent group: Che Guevara, Mao Tse-tung, and Frantz Fanon have almost nothing in common with the liberals' past.

The media are producing a generation of middle-echelon leaders who do not find the old past to be useful for their reportage. While dissenters regularly point to the complete take-over of the mass media by repressive and manipulative forces, it is apparent that on many levels there is quiet rebellion from within. Scores of cameramen, reporters, and photographers who covered the war in Vietnam came to reject their government's sense of what was credible or reportable. They were repulsed by national military policies. They chose camera angles, subjects, and subject matter which helped present an alternative view of the war.

In the urban crisis, many editors and reporters began to identify with the problems of the overlooked people who had moved from victim status to assertive and aggressive status. Their critics argued that the Black Power leaders, for example, were products of the media: they had no following to speak of apart from reporters. These writers and interviewers came to see that society as it had been put together offered nothing to those who were left out in urban America and they worked to present an alternative picture. They developed, along the way, a dissenting conscience. The media, overall, may have remained timid and trivializing; but not a few of their employees worked to fashion a new conscience and consciousness and found little appealing in the consensus or the tradition.

Still another group, and one which will receive attention in this book, includes religious leadership. The laity had often pioneered in the effort to see religion speak meaningfully to the modern world. But much of the more extreme rejection of the past came from clerical leadership in church and synagogue. In a specialized society, the clergy were functionally and emotionally prepared to step out of their traditional roles as assenters and to take on dissenting tasks. They were mobile; they were chartered to study the society and the quality of persons in it; they were called to criticize, prophesy, and innovate.

The clergy have often been seen as the custodians of tradition in society, with good reason. Not only is religion often a stabilizing and conservative force, but in America it also was the locale for an undeclared game of politics between clerics and laity. In a voluntary society, where religious institutions are dependent upon the good will of clienteles, that good will cannot be pushed or tested too much. Support drops and people lose confidence in the stable. But in the 1960s significant minorities of the clerical and lay leadership moved into the front of race and peace activities, and almost nowhere was there a controversial societal movement that was not led by sisters or reverends or rabbis.

This leadership often found that it could become involved only through apparent rejection of the tradition. Sometimes the rejection was seen by the society as bordering on the bizarre. How could it be that people called theo-logians (speakers about God) could speak of the impossibility of God-talk or even of the death of God—and still go on being theologians? How could Christians, and thus God-believers, stop believing, but instead of being merely agnostics or doubters, style themselves Christian atheists? How could people in the Catholic tradition claim to take their cue only from the future and to bypass or express distaste for most of what had been spoken in the apparently useless past? *How* will be answered, in part, in later chapters of this book. *That* they did these things hardly needs chronicling.

To this suggestive catalogue of dissenters, for whom the conventional past is apparently useless, it would be possible to add many others. Some are individual entrepreneurs, people who through their private reading or reflection have come to feel cut off from the way society measures its past and present.

One could cite the groups of hippies and yippies, people who would "tune in, turn on, and drop out"; those who could say, "We are the children our parents warned us about"[8]: the flower-children, the mind-blowing, consciousness-expanding, drug-experimenting, love-in, and be-in types. While they have been going through a series of readily obsolete cultural styles and fads, there seemed to be continuity in their sense of rejection of the wisdom in the Western and Christian traditions.[9] Many of them turned readily and overtly to the East and to various Eastern religions, philosophies, cults, and pseudo-religions for temporary inspiration. When they seized on moments of the Christian tradition—by appropriating something of Jesus, or St. Francis, or Jacob Boehme—they would do so outside of the historical contexts in which these leaders had first appeared.

Clearly, there were plenty of rejectors; there were enough living minds which found the past largely useless; there were numerous spirits that claimed to be oriented only to the now or the future. They had not yet all found each other, though individually they had been given considerable attention by a nervous society.

Nowhere did the sense of a useless past seem more obvious than in the realm of religion. While not all members of the society would turn to this area with curiosity or fear or hope—religion seems to be located safely in a quiet separate precinct, apart from the crossroads of power—others were coming to see that in it the rejection of tradition was particularly strong. While much of it appeared in reformist contexts, at other times it seemed to be the voice only of those who were groping for the new without having much of a plan or program. In both cases, one could prove that the rejection of the past was not complete: the spokesmen may have spoken against the whole past in the interest of selective elements. Thus Thomas Altizer argued that American theology was now free from the past,[10] could be wholly new and fresh—yet he documented his own case and drew inspiration from nineteenth-century writers like Blake, Nietzsche, Hegel, and Dostoyevsky. Catholics who rejected Thomas reached at least to Teilhard (who also belongs to the past) or to other points of inspiration out of the past. But the intention of many religious leaders was to incite what they called a revolution full of rejection and a thirst for the new.

C. S. Lewis has written that those who do not know history will be victims of recent bad history. The religious revolutionaries seem, to their critics, to be attacking all of religious history when actually they may be (whether they themselves know it or not!) only attacking the recent—nineteenth-century—past. A study of the dimensions of the revolution will make this clear, even as it will not minimize that sense that the immediate past is useless.

The revolution in religion, symbolic of so many other changes, can best be expressed in a simple picture: it has meant the movement of religious affairs from the religion page of the metropolitan newspapers to the front page. During the religious revival of the 1950s, editors of newspapers enlarged the religion sections of the Saturday newspapers. They reported on fund-raising events, eccentric sermon titles, cornerstone layings, confirmations, and revivalist rallies. As the revival of interest in this kind of thing waned, that section of newspapers diminished again. Poll-takers a decade later found that two-thirds of the American people felt that religion was declining in influence in human affairs. The reaction was understandable, but in part it resulted from people's inability to resituate themselves in their analysis of the role of religion.

They did not know to look on the front page. There for a decade religious change was one of the major stories. India and Pakistan fought over Hindu and Muslim tensions; Catholics and many kinds of Buddhist contended in Vietnam; the Arab-Israeli War was drenched in religious matters; in Latin America the

Church stood on both sides of political life. In the United States the Supreme Court regularly had to rule on religious issues; the faith of Presidential candidates was often a topic for discussion; the clergy provided leadership for the civil rights cause; even radical theologians made page one. Whatever ultimate disposition society would make of religious issues, in the 1960s it was clear that people were seeing a greater, not a lesser, exposure to front-page religion.

This picture represents another dimension of the change. Religion was moving from a private sector to a public one where, at least in the appropriated recent past, it had seemed to be a stranger. While the Hebrew Scriptures and the New Testament had spoken of the act of being saved as a social one, of the People of God and the New People of God or the Body of Christ; although Christian history had normally seen the involvement of the whole Church as a body in societal formation and change, the early-modern settlement had called for putting religion in a box. In Emile Durkheim's fundamental formula,[11] many areas of life that had once belonged to the religious spokesman or the priest fell into the hands of specialists in a complex society. In this division of labor, the modern clergy were assigned the care of private, personal, familial, and leisure life. The society at large, once this bargain was struck, spoke respectfully of religion: you stay out of the way in your corner, it said in effect, and we will honor and support you. Many religious spokesmen came to regard this division as normative for Christianity.

Others experienced that the little box or the little corner was itself being reduced. The marital counselor and the psychiatrist crowded the familial and personal areas; the change in Sabbath observance in a two-car and one-boat culture chipped away at the leisure time. Perhaps because of the status crisis but for sure because of a new vision of the mandate of religion and the needs of society, leadership started to break out of the segregated areas. The clergy and lay agents wanted to have the People of God present as a movement or force in race relations, economic life, housing concerns, international affairs, and wherever else matters of "the other six days" were faced decisively.

Such a movement, it can be demonstrated, was a return to the characteristic life of the Christian past. The point is that the agents of change spoke as if what they were doing was new and had to be done in rejection of that useless past which had dislocated religion. They were then able to point out that in the modern political world there was no nonpolitical place to stand or position to hold. "Not to take a stand on an important issue meant taking a stand." The churches which would not speak up for an issue of change could be counted on by powerful forces as representatives of the status quo.

Other dimensions of the religious change can be seen in the light of this religion-page to front-page, private to public movement. The public devotional past seemed to be pointless, so far as the agents of religious change were concerned. They saw the need for a move from the devotional to the substantive to be urgent. That is, they were resentful of the useless past with its Presidential prayer breakfasts, Inaugural Day devotions, Little League and Garden Club invocations, and the thousands of other ways in which the clergy were expected to speak without being allowed to contribute. When the Supreme Court ruled out prayer and devotion in the schools, poll-takers found that about four out of five Americans were critical of the court. People found the ceremonial role of religion to be safe and traditional. Much religious leadership applauded the Court and resisted potential Constitutional change, finding that the uprooting from the tradition made it possible for them to address society once again instead of merely speaking past society and "to God in prayer."

The revolution was a movement from security to risk. The two-centuries-old tradition had charged the religious leadership with contentment in its assigned place. They were expected to cater for favor and financial contributions, to care for the endowments and prerogatives, the prestige and repute of religious institutions. When the change came, there was risk. The old politicking between the pulpit and the pew was threatened. Old doctrines, dogmas, and institutions were almost casually called into question. Inherited modes of worship did not seem to speak directly and there was wild experiment. Clerics were not always mindful of

the toes on which they stepped, the purse strings they were clos-
ing, the grocery bills they were mounting without visible means
of support.

The public was also conscious of the rejection of the denominational tradition on the part of the new religious leaders. The
Ecumenical Movement still received public attention, but it meant
little to the new activists, to seminarians, and to the radical religious thinkers. To them, the attempts to unite the churches carried over too much of the inherited logic of divided Christian
life. Committees of representative traditions met and studied and
negotiated. They gave and they took, they politicked and com-
promised, they improvised and accommodated—with the intent
to merge and reformulate. But to the newer agents of change the
achievements seemed minimal, marginal, and beside the point.
The revolutionary religionists had already found each other
across the sectarian, confessional, and denominational lines, and
the traditional achievements of negotiated settlements, cease-fires,
truces, and rapprochements offered little for their urgent needs
and demands.

So the churches were moving from consent to dissent in the
larger society; no longer content to be the antique-shop dusters
or the baptizers of a culture that had already made up its mind
about what was important, they were resentful of the immediate
past, incautious about the tradition. In their desire to move people from religious ghettos to interaction, they were not curious
about those who had built the old walls and took little hope from
the unsuccessful pioneers who had battered against them in the
past. In choosing to move from a religious to a more worldly
role in society, they found that almost all the words in their little
black books were colored by unworldly, otherworldly references
which held little promise for them.

The clergy who had wanted only to save people out of the
world could criticize the society for having become too independent, too worldly, too far removed from sacral norms: in doing so, they were like blond parents criticizing their children for
being blond. By accepting the traditional modern role they had

settled for life in the safe little box or corner. Those who wanted to break out had to fight or ignore the past.

To those who protested such a move, the agents of change could argue that failure to reject and to innovate meant buying the terms of a diseased and dying world; it meant stagnation and death. These may have represented a statistical minority. They could not well have claimed to speak *for* the Church,[12] if that meant counting votes and casting a ballot on the basis of majorities. But they were trying to speak to the Church and, through it, to the world.

Many readers of these pages may not have seen all the dimensions of this revolution. They are overwhelmed by the heavy weight of the past and tradition on local churches and denominations; they see and feel little change. They speak for a majority vision, and have to be reckoned with. But in a Church where the three and The Twelve have mattered in mission, numbers do not dominate. Already those who have rejected one past and thus stood at the side of other dissenters can point to achievements that have begun to mean change in society, and they move on—not always with guidelines or landmarks—to build on those achievements which have emboldened them already.

2

The Useful Search for a Future

$\mathcal{T}$he power of numbers stands
with those who represent the consensus or tradition of the immediate past. Power *stands*. But, as Horace Bushnell put it pithily
a century ago, "power *moves* in the direction of hope."[13] Hoping
is only one mode of dealing with the future, but Bushnell's saying is a clue to the whole range of future orientations of the recent
past.

Along with the rejection of the whole tradition or at least of
the immediate past, and during the time when large sectors of the
society find it impossible to relate to the consensus based on that
past, recent years have seen an obsession with the future. People
have dreamed, seen visions, written Utopias, drawn plans, pre-
scribed programs, predicted, prophesied, guessed, and played futures-games with a vengeance. It may be argued that all responsible people have always had an eye on the future, but for many
reasons there has been an increase of interest in the subject.

The investment in the future can be read as a sign of restlessness, of neurotic anxiety on the part of people who have given up on complexity. It may be the luxury of the affluent cultures, where the raw material and inspiration for planning are present in abundance. It may be a sick attempt to escape from history, to express ingratitude to the past, to assert the pride of novelty. It may be the mark of grim, late Puritan-Protestant pursuit—or a healthy mark of maturity. In any case, its many evidences need documentation.

In France Bertrand de Jouvenel and his *Futuribles* group chart a variety of possibilities. In the United States the American Academy of Arts and Sciences has chartered a Committee on the Year 2000 under Daniel Bell; it is expected to prepare numerous potential futures.[14] One of the best known of the endeavors has come from the Rand Corporation and the Hudson Institute, where what can be known about the immediate past is programmed into a chart of possibilities for the future of production or of warfare. The computer-programmers who serve industry and business by trying to organize various potentials have been described as *The New Utopians*.[15]

Some of the more visionary attention-getters have tried some weird coinages to suggest basic changes in the whole environment and chemical or biological make-up of man: we are called to foresee life in the *Dybosphere*.[16] Short-range planners have a well-established place in a world that moves by stock market changes, economic gambles, production schedules, and consumer possibilities.

Full-orbed Utopians have appeared on the scene, moved by religious or other visions to depict the outlines of a forthcoming Kingdom of God among men, a Peaceable Kingdom of right and good and beauty. Revolutionaries in the political realm describe the good life which presumably will rise after they have been able to blow up or pull down the old establishment and power centers.

Science fiction is greeted with new curiosity as one of the means of creating imaginative or terror-inspiring possibilities for the future when scientific discovery proceeds apace. Finally, there has been an outburst, in the middle of an age that styles itself scientific, of crystal-ball gazing, horoscope-reading, tea-leaf analysis, and other forms of prophecy based on omens, signs, and superstitions. Historians treat all these attempts with a healthy measure of skepticism or a measure of healthy skepticism. They have seen how little has come from the Utopias of the past and have no reason to trust the astrologers of their own time, given the bad record of predictors in the past. But they are not left wholly out of the business or game of dealing with the future and, as we shall see, make many of their judgments about the past in the light of a distinctive approach to the future. How to develop that approach is the question.

An immediate temptation is to try to dazzle by citing the fantastic elements of any envisionable future. The more dramatic of these have to do with population projections: if the world continues to grow at its present pace, before many centuries pass people will be standing on each other's heads. The technological future serves to titillate. One can speak of the day when all the written knowledge of the world could be condensed in a pinhead-sized capsule and retrieved from it. Appropriate gasps are anticipated and in order. One can extrapolate on the basis of present trends and awe people with pictures of the future of the knowledge explosion, until the day comes when all knowledge doubles within a year or a month or a day—each spokesman is allowed his own term in the war of escalation.

One can play the game by indulging in latter-day Teilhardian or Darwinian speculation, and speak of the emergence of a future two million years from now. (The historian might well argue that the next two years will be hardest. The enlightened Frenchwoman, when told by a high cleric that the patron saint of Paris walked a hundred miles, head in hand, after decapitation, remarked that the first steps, in such a promenade, are the hardest![17]) Some of this future-of-evolution talk appears in scientific guise but is also merely fictional speculation.

The futures-game has inspired a great deal of jargon and pseudo-profound talk. Jargon rises because the future will inspire possibilities for which present-day terms hardly suffice, and because many gamesmen seem to feel that their talk will acquire profundity through the accession of difficult and eccentric language. Some cells and centers of Christian renewal, moved by rejection of the past, have devoted themselves almost wholly to the development of such a revolutionary lingo. The listener, who is expected to be entranced or terrorized, finds it possible to shrug off the whole effort; a friend full of common sense offers the put-down, "I never agree or disagree with anything any of them ever says." The advantage of such future chatter is that one can so easily sound impressive and profound, in full confidence that he cannot be checked out—the future events have not yet occurred—and with at least some uneasy sense that what he is saying will have been long forgotten by the time the future stage begins to unfold.

The historian, the politician, and the agent of change when they deal with the future may profit from the more fanciful and fantastic versions, but they will normally attempt a feet-on-the-ground approach. For they know that in a complex, political, and technological society, the future abhors a vacuum. While they may well follow the Biblical injunctions not to be anxious about the tomorrows, they know that they cannot avoid preparing and planning. In the technical order, it is impossible to make a contribution without the programming of possibilities years in advance. In medicine, research is related to explicit and detailed programs designed to help bring about breakthroughs, discovery, and cures. In politics, one is always aware of caprice and contingency, but he takes positions and lines up delegates with an eye on the future. Those who would be agents of change know that they are not in a position to abandon all talk about the future to the far-out groups.

The future-obsession has been less prominent in less developed societies. Where people live by the rhythms of harvest and seedtime, planning beyond four seasons has seldom involved more than building bigger granaries as a protection against drought and famine. In underpopulated cultures people did not have to envision population trends. In a purer, less crowded world, they did not have to begin to project pictures of a wholly polluted atmosphere or corrupt environment—and then to prevent its development. The crowded and complex society allows no such luxury of waiting.

One mistake of the futurists of the recent past inheres in their tendency to elide from their concern with the technological order, where future-projection is fairly well-grounded, to the humanistic realm, with its talk of beliefs and norms and values. Technological projection is the basis for much of the urgent future talk, and when it is recalled, there is a meaningful judgment against some of the romantic futurists, including many political revolutionaries.

Because technology and the machine have played a big part in the development of a suppressing establishment and a repressive culture, some revolutionaries have contended for a future free of cities and machines and computers. The village model is once again pictured as workable; people go back to arts and crafts, tilling and digging. Yet when one questions them in detail to see whether their rejection of the technological future is complete, he discerns many notable gaps. For example, they picture modern hospitals as something which can enlarge the range of human possibilities (though they, and I, may well engage in a critique of the impersonality of much in modern hospitaldom). They picture the fruits of medical technology as an element of the good life for people in American inner cities and in the villages of the Third World. Yet it is logically and technologically impossible to isolate one element out of the complexity: X-ray, drug, and surgical research are interlocked with every other kind of research.

Attempts to envision a future without complexity in the world of things seems to be beside the point, a frivolous and retrogressive or nostalgic exercise. They point to an urgent and legitimate question, however: "Is a humane technological society possible, and how is it to be achieved?" With Jacques Ellul[18] we may claim merely to report on the inevitable development of technology and of the inevitable dehumanization and enslaving that go along with it; more creative is the attempt to move beyond reportage into major attempts to minimize the harm done the human by such an order. A fateful ambiguity attends that order:

it can enlarge or trivialize life. The human factor remains the realm of choice.

When people do affirm technology, as many of the hard Utopians of the recent past have done, they often move easily into the humanistic realm: thus Thomas Edison is often quoted to the general effect that what the hand of man can create the mind and spirit of man can control. That has to be demonstrated and proved: the case remains open. Once again, there is a fateful ambiguity, a dual and open development in which human purpose plays its part.

Confused by the conflicting signs presented by a culture marked by "rapidation,"[19] contenders over the future have offered two opposite scripts within the space of a half dozen years.

In their search for a usable future, some gamesmen in the early 1960s resorted to Utopia. Knowing that audacity was called for and inspired by the confidence that man was prevailing, they pictured a realm of possibility to which our culture was tending. The technological and the humane orders were converging to create a world wherein conflict may remain but in which it would be productive of good. There men would learn to embrace the works of their hands, to affirm the human city. The fundamental human model for this was the cool, worldly, problem-solving, practical man. Man in control. He was now orbiting the world, probing the depths of the sea. Aided by all the disciplines, he could foresee problems and program his way through or past them. This was to be a society of affluence, abundance, leisure, and meaningful human relations.

When the Utopian scripts were provided in a religious or a Christian context, there seemed to be even more basis for optimism. At last, the ancient word about man having dominion and control over nature was coming to pass. The elemental spirits of superstition were to be annihilated. Lordship was to be asserted; God was where the action is; the new creation might very well be Metropolis.

Legacies of the religious past were to be rejected along with other useless and enslaving matters. Visions of "original sin" or a "predestining God," visions which had only recently been resurrected and transformed modishly by the new orthodox religious thinkers, were once again to be purged. Man would not be haunted again by omens; he did not need to visit the sanctuaries or make his peace with the gods. The gloomy existentialists who had won their way in some parts of the Western world obviously did not speak to the swingers and cool men of the new emerging world. The children of affluence took to optimism as an agreeable philosophy of history. Problems remained: Utopia was not a simplistic picture. But these problems would be resolved through mopping-up operations; beachheads had been established everywhere.

In ethics, John F. Kennedy and Martin Luther King embodied something of the new style, mingling political charism, religious reminiscence, and personal style with a strong pragmatic sense: the good men were winning. A Great Society was offered. In the churches, Pope John was now in command; the Vatican Council was bringing the Catholic Church up to date. Religious thinkers had come to apply themselves to real problems of real people and not to the realm of spooks and of angels. Idols were being toppled, devils forgotten, gods killed, and man would be free and open.

Pope John died. The two Kennedys and Martin Luther King were assassinated. Watts burned. Vietnam proved to be a moral, political, and military nightmare. The Great Society crumbled before the foundations were finished. People spoke of a society "sick unto death."

In a you-cannot-win-them-all spirit the futurists went back to their homework, to come up with an alternative scenario. Some were silent. Others who in the earlier 1960s were offering Utopia, the realm of fulfilled good, now envisioned Armageddon, the realm of conflict, final battle, and the end, as the only possibility. For some the new scenario was born only of defeat and frustration; it held a nihilist tinge and attracted masochists and self-flagellants. But for others it was designed as a script which might inspire alternative courses of action. "Brother, there is still time."

Armageddon could be classified among the searches for a usable future only in the hands of those who cited it to inspire action. But the action now pictured was no longer cool, pragmatic, problem-solving. Now it had new mythic and mystical elements; neglected symbols were reinvoked. The Dionysian elements of religion and the violent overtones of politics were evoked. The call came to disrupt, burn, destroy, bring down the existing order —in the belief that perhaps something new might come to take its place on the field of Armageddon.

This script tied in with the destructive side of technology. Edison was wrong: man could create but could not or did not have the will to control. The neo-orthodox theologians were wrong, but only in that their views of the human state were not gloomy enough. God is dead. The Church is dead. These had been asserted in Utopia as marks of human fulfillment; now they were invoked to remind men of the desperation of their condition: the fire this time was present. People were called upon to despair of politics and the democratic process, to abandon legal maneuvering and rational argument, to reject the realm of "repressive tolerance"[20] and the quest for therapy between people. The Church was called to abandon the progressivist logic that was inspiring renewal. Now people were either to revert to gloom or drop out or dance on graves or celebrate in spite of . . .

Both Utopia and Armageddon were false and futile scripts; both lead and led to misguided action, frustration, and immobilization. To say the least, when both are asserted by the same persons or groups of people within a few years of each other, there is every reason for their audiences to lose confidence in them.

If the prophets failed in the decade of the search for a usable future, some lessons at least can be retrieved. The first of these is that history eludes apotheosis. It does not turn into God. It is not all malleable to human purpose, including people of good will. The tragic in life will not go away simply because people deride the holders of a tragic sense of life. Progress can be thwarted. Boredom sets in, even in Utopia. The human story could end and, eventually, will end. Men die.

Because of the sudden change in atmosphere and mood among the futurists, a new determinism and a kind of fatalism set in.

Utopia or the Kingdom of God did not come: why bother? The old determinism, made up of some Christian and some Islamic elements, called for human passivity in the face of divine initiative. What will be will be. The Lord wills it. It included some dimensions of Eastern religion, where the arrow of history had not been discerned so readily as in the West, and thus where adaptation to the cycles of history or to fate was pictured as creative.

The worldly theologies and progressivist Utopias were designed to counter that kind of determinism. They were designed to deliver the *coup de grâce* to all such forces in history. They would defatalize and desacralize an imprisoning and ghostly universe. They would dispel mystery. They drew on the wisdom and prophecy of the great bearded men of the nineteenth century, the god-killing Marxes, Nietzsches, Darwins, and Freuds, and then related the godless terrain to new optimistic forces. But then, only a few years later, men were reverting to a new kind of determinism.

The new determinism looked at the worlds of population and pollution, nuclear threat and world revolution, and said, in effect: Man can do nothing. From the viewpoint of work for the human future, one could say that the worst thing to do would be to provide a theological rationale for such determinism. The second worst would be to ask for a new swing of the pendulum to still another Utopian charter. The one says that man can do nothing; the other, that he can do everything. Both have been disproven within the decade when the two scripts were resurrected as searches for a usable future.

If men are not to abandon themselves to the future in a mindless way and if, on the other hand, they go wrong with Utopias and Armageddons, it is important to ask just how they might deal creatively with the future. Serendipity, gambles, luck, drift, and chance will continue to have their part. Some *bricolage*,[21] some jack-of-all-tradesmanship, may play its part. But it is also profitable to outline some rational, planned approaches. For this task, Daniel Bell[22] has offered twelve modes of dealing with prediction or with the future. What follows is an extremely free adaptation of some of these motifs, designed to relate only to the argument of this book.

The first is prediction. The search for a usable future is carried on by many who, after having surveyed the past and discerning rhythms or cycles there—or on some other basis from guesswork up—make a stab at depicting a future. The critical historian has nothing to do with this approach. Nothing in his training, methods, or materials gives him a warrant for predicting; his studies reveal the fate of prediction in the past. If he is Christian, nothing in his faith gives him a charter for confidence in dealing with the detail of the future. He knows nothing of such detail.

More grounded is the approach which follows trends. One can make an effort at future planning on the common-sense basis of drawing graphs and charts, following them into the future with all due allowance for every kind of foreseeable factor. Such an approach is helpful in business, industrial, and technological areas; for example, on this basis one can make meaningful projections of future populations, numbers of anticipated housing starts or college enrollments, or similar possibilities. For short-range practical matters this is the most convenient and helpful approach.

People approach the future with philosophies of history. On the basis of revelation, speculation, metaphysics, or pure hunch, they devise an outlook which assumes a kind of knowledge of the outcome of history.[23] Without some such view of outcomes, ends, or fulfillments, it is difficult to picture how a philosophy of history can be developed. For such a philosophy inveterately makes comments upon *the* meaning of history or meaning *in* history. Yet such meaning cannot be discerned by the ordinary analyst, for the returns are not all yet in. Only by having some way of viewing the outcome of history as if it has already occurred can men speak of the meaning of history by reference to events before the end.

The authors of recent Utopias and Armageddons have often been unwitting (and sometimes witting) philosophers of history, though they have not always laid bare their bases for foreseeing certain specific outcomes in history. They may not always be explicitly religious or theological: the Marxists, for example, deal with the future as if it had already occurred, "knowing" the outcome (as, one might say, in the "classless society"). It has been said that they had no divinity but that they wore and wear theological spectacles. The historian need not attack the philosophers of history; he has only to point out what they are trying to do and to make their audiences aware of the kind of knowledge which is being offered.

Still another method of approaching a usable future is to deal with the obsessive interests of a society. Thus America gives every evidence of having to deal with the racial picture until it comes to the Utopia of solution or the Armageddon of Final Solution or some more probable intervening course. One cannot predict which of the outcomes might develop, but he makes some contribution by locating where energies toward solution will be directed. One can assume without much fear of contradiction that the society will somehow spend more energy on this question than it might on how to have *aggiornamento* in the Knights of Pythias. The fact of a new kind of revolutionary nationalism is an obsessive issue which is altering the Cold War mentality and with which there are many reasons to believe the society will have to wrestle for years to come.

Daniel Bell also points to searches for a usable future concentrating on certain requirements of the system. Thus America has a Constitution, a party system, a sequence of elections. While it is possible that these all can be overthrown in an age of revolution and dissent, short of such overthrowing, one narrows the range of future-projection somewhat by locating possibilities within the framework. He can know little of detail. Americans on November 21, 1963, "knew" who the next Democratic candidate would be, as they also knew until a Sunday night in the spring of 1968 when President Johnson withdrew. But if such detail eludes them, they can at least concentrate energies on filling some roles and spots within a party system every two or four years.

They may seek futures by looking at the sources of power: in some ages one might advise, "Bet on Establishment!" At others, one can see so much upheaval that he can urge, "Bet on dissent!"

In the modern world one can usually bet on the bureaucratic continuity, on the potency of the oncoming generation, on a military establishment.

From the point of view of agents of change, however, probably the most helpful approach is the writing of alternative futures, disposable or revisable scripts and scenarios, and dealing with a variety of "as ifs" in the human future. These are imaginative projections based on a range of possibilities. This method, in the eyes of many, might seem tainted or might look at best like the seizing of the good from the very jaws of evil, for it is often associated with the work of Herman Kahn and others who have worked out alternative futures of escalation and toward thermonuclear warfare. Whatever its source or most sophisticated area of development, there is potential in the approach which forms paradigms or models of every kind of future possibility and follows through with sets of plausible fictions. If this happens, then what do we do?

Such an approach, while it includes the element of fantasy ("as if") or of fiction is not blind or mindless. It includes a reckoning with all possible details based on present knowledge and precedent. One attractive feature: it is not merely determinist and can be a stimulant to the imagination. Over against the passivity of some of the disciples of Teilhard de Chardin, who allow for a rather relentless unfolding of an inevitable future, it sides with the revisionists like Raymond Nogar,[24] who see development in the hands of men who are and must be fully free, fully intelligent, fully human, fully responsible. Father Nogar quite properly adds to his vision of the human future the distinctive note: "Without God, man can in no way be fully free and intelligent in shaping his destiny." This avenue toward the future builds upon what is legitimate in all the other modes of dealing with the future just described.

When such an understanding of alternative scripts or scenarios is introduced, the critical historian or analyst is freed from some of the limitations which the logic of tenses ordinarily imposes on him. He is no longer restricted only to waiting to see what comes about so that he can have his first word, as a historian (who has nothing to say about events until they have occurred!). Instead,

he is free to toss out imaginative projections and then to take a
responsible part in seeing them come to fulfillment. Historical
judgments based upon such stabs into the future are inevitable.
How does one judge that Hitler was "bad"? Must he make a
case metaphysically or revelationally every time he wants to talk
about Hitler? Or must he remain so neutral that his reader never
finds out whether there was something wrong with Hitler? He
makes his judgments on the basis of alternative views of the outcome of history. He bets on the human venture, and judges well
those who allow for fully free and open, fully intelligent and
human development; he is critical of those who thwart them.
Such an approach is better than resorting to blind chance. In
Professor George Allan's version: such an involvement is less
surgical and ascetic or antiseptic than is that of the purely analytical historian; it is less "neat," but more productive of consequences.

Later this approach will be applied in detail to some urgent
questions in the field of religion. Is the human future to be godless, as many recent observers have argued? Or is man inevitably
to be seen as godly, and particular religions then must relate only
to the better and worse means of being godly? The historian cannot answer: he does not know the end or outcome of history. He
does not rule out the godless possibilities in a previously sacral
understanding or the godly possibilities in a world that is called
secular.

Such an approach is not a disguised apology for the faith. It
does nothing at all to prove or disprove the existence of God or
the solution to the riddle of existence. Many of its major implications have to do with the realm of action. "If I believe, then
this is how I will act." "I act as if this possibility may come into
play and that someone may be thwarted if I take the action instead of remaining passive and inert." Men can then act "as if"
human history is worthwhile, or "as if" God is the power of the
future. Normally, they will do this only if they already have believed it to be true; the investment is too expensive and the demands on energy too strenuous for play actors or mere wagerers.

The use of imaginative projections or the designing of alternative futures can help in the overcoming of malaise or frustration after the sense of exhaustion or the peddling of cocksure visions of the future. The paradigms come from the tradition—where else can one gain the materials for designing or writing them?— but they need not spell out in detail the inevitable fulfillments implied by terms like Utopia or Armageddon. They call for human response and responsibility. They help free people from the dead hand of the past without building up so much frustration over the lack of fulfillment in the future.

In effect, one "bounces off" the screen of the future some images gained from what has prevailed, from present tendency, and from what one might wish to see prevailing in the future. Then he calls people to try to live out the consequences of the steps needed to bring about such a situation. All this is more modest than prediction, crystal-ball gazing, prophecy, or engaging in the writing of all-inclusive philosophies of history. But it helps overcome inevitabilism and determinism in ways that they may not. It does not build up illusions and ask men to march for assured causes with assured outcomes in mind. In a most serious way, proposed participants are informed in advance that they are playing a game whose outcome is anything but assured. In spite of the best-made plans, everything can go wrong.

At the very least, such a futures game avoids the necessity of speaking breathlessly about the future, dazzling by projection, confusing by jargon, or deluding by promising more than can be delivered. It serves as a lever to help people free themselves from recent bad history. There is in it no disguised metaphysic, no assumption that has to be smoked out and exposed to view. Its assumption is patent: people are invited to see how affairs would stand if they took part in bringing about this or that consequence.

In *The Meaning of History*,[25] Nicholas Berdyaev has described a dialectic of history not too far removed from the argument of this chapter. He foresaw moments in history like our own, when the direct integral and organic experience of some settled historical order was being lost. The static age is over; people find that annals and chronicles do not speak to them because the power implied in such accounts offers no promise or hope to them. He spoke, second, of a period of fateful and menacing schism and disruption, when the old established order is being challenged and is giving away. The result: the knowing subject does not feel himself directly and wholly a part of the historical object. Here speculation (Utopia, Armageddon, futures-games) is born. There may be a great sense of schism in the soul in such a period.

Then comes a third period, which may again be called "historical." Berdyaev's picture may seem speculative, too general, and somewhat Hegelian. But those who do not wish to become mixed up in speculation can see the development of the first two steps in the recent past. Whether or not the third comes to play would, in this argument, depend upon whether men wanted it to—at least in part. The "historical" moment may not yet have arrived. For Berdyaev that moment meant the devising of philosophy of history, through a particularly acute consciousness, an aptitude for speculation and aspiration toward the mysteries of the riddle of history.

The search for a usable future offered in this chapter remains much more modest and more cool than Berdyaev's. It allows for the participation by people who do not share speculative mentalities. Their acute consciousness can be directed toward games and projects which matter-of-fact men can enjoy.

They may disdain Berdyaev's speculative consciousness and yet get the fruits of what it is to which he strives. The sense of schism and disruption is overcome or at least creatively channeled. With Jacob Burckhardt, they may find that philosophy of history is for them an impossibility, a centaur, a contradiction in terms ("for history co-ordinates, and hence is unphilosophical, while philosophy subordinates, and hence is unhistorical"). This does not mean that they have to abandon passion for Burckhardt's subject. They play their futures-games, starting out "from the one point accessible to us, the one eternal center of all things —man, suffering, striving, doing, as he is and was and ever shall be."[26] By their act, they contribute to his striving and possibly to his achieving.

3

The Half-False Prophecy

The search for a usable future has led Western religious thinkers to undertake the outlining of the most ambitious reworking of religious themes and forms in the last millennium and a half. A discussion of their endeavor, with its limits and its gains, should have an obvious interest for Christian believers or those brought up in the Christian tradition. Those who have never been part of this faith or its community may, at first at least, feel left out or repelled. Why should the doings of Western European and Anglo-American professional religious thinkers concern them?

At first hearing, this rejection sounds more than plausible and serves as a reminder of the actual power and potential of the tradition and its recent translators. The crisis in the humanities[27] has left the theologian and the other humanist scholars in a curious position. They are the "clerks," and few look to them today for cognitive matters, for the stuff out of which they can learn about the universe. One turns to the scientist for such knowl-

edge. Only in luxury does one turn to the clerk, with considerable lack of certainty about what he has to offer.

More reasonably the nonreligious person could express curiosity about the thought of the church politician. He at least
commands control of large numbers of people who have certain
sets of interests they might express at the ballot box. Their views
on housing, race, war and peace, education, or other matters
might actually have an impact on how a community is run and
how power is set up and dispersed. The theologian is once-
removed from the church politician and his clientele. His books
are read by the few who have special tastes.

Most embarrassing of all, the theologian is expected to speak
about God. Yet great numbers of people centuries ago made up
their minds about the subject: they regard it as extraneous or
superfluous. It gets in no one's way and neither adds to nor de-
tracts from most ways of going about the day's work or fulfilling
human purpose. Therefore when the theologian opens his mouth
on his allotted subject matter, he cuts himself off from all but
the backward-looking and obtuse few who have not yet liberated
themselves from such modes of thinking. To put it as bluntly as
possible: the religious thinker is not very big on the contemporary
scene, especially when his impact is compared to that of the
general, the financier, the racial leader, or the politician.

All true. Yet something may also be said for the social importance of discerning what it is that recent theologians have been
after. They speak out of and to a community that is world-wide
in scope and which numbers up to one-fourth of the human race.
For all its division, its shortcoming, its halfheartedness, this community does inspire millions of people to loyalty and sacrifice;
many of them through it view their destiny and the ultimate
issues of life. Its shape and stance has had a great impact on
many cultures and even now one cannot envision Latin America
passing through its change without facing the power and thought
of the Church. Europe has so much of Christian thought webbed
into its fabric that change in the thought will pull at the whole
fabric. In the United States the majority of people are affiliated
with religious institutions and the vast majority claim some

identification with the main tenets of Christianity. Change in that community will have some sort of effect on the world at large.

Within the religious community the theologian or theorist plays a changing role. Once upon a time most theology was written in episcopal or monastic centers. In the modern world, it occurs chiefly in the academy. Classically, this has meant at the university, in exposure to other modes of thought. When the universities underwent change during the nineteenth century and when they were often studiously uncongenial to theology, the seminaries developed as centers for training of ministry and doing religious theorizing. But in the recent past, the seminary has taken on university style of thought; the professors are trained at universities; the seminaries are again huddling up to and often integrating with the programs of universities. In short, the gap is again narrowing and most serious theology is conditioned by a pluralist environment.

Meanwhile, the theologian has begun to play a somewhat different role in the life of the Christian community than he did in the recent past. Once expected to be the caretaker of the assured verities, he is now charged with finding ways to relate the faith to a world of change. He is expected to be in the advance guard of religious activity. Vatican Council II made this position of the theologian clear: he whispered into the ear of the bishop, who did the voting. The vast changes effected in Catholicism were widely attributed to the impact of the professional theologian.

The world of public media has also discovered a new potency in religious thought. In part this has been the result of a generation of giants in thought: names like Martin Buber, Jacques Maritain, Albert Schweitzer, Paul Tillich, Reinhold Niebuhr, and Karl Barth belong to characters so colorful and prepossessing that reporters and disseminators of opinion could ignore them only at their peril. More than this, the media have learned that religious thinkers have a double impact on society. For one thing, they relate through changes they effect in their particular communities and churches. For another, they speak not to but out of these communities. One might argue that theologians have nothing to talk about apart from the language and achievement of particular communities. In short: power is related to change in theological circles.

Already this change has had an effect on thought about birth control and family planning, personal morality and the sexual ethos, business mores and military activity, racial affairs, political life, and personal style. People who study the nuances of expression on the part of Black Power advocates, "the New York Jewish intellectual establishment," or Students for a Democratic Society, may sometimes overlook them in something so taken for granted and protean as the world-wide Christian community, but they remain significant.

This apology or citing of a power potential has been designed as an introduction to one form of the search for a usable future, the most ambitious new theological program in some years. Here it will be sympathetically criticized and seen as a half-false prophecy (which, by positive thinkers, can be read as a half-true prophecy!). The central, dominant, and almost obsessive concern of recent religious thinkers has had to do with the milieu, subject matter, and intention of theology as being captured in the word "worldly." This must be examined for the ways in which it has disguised a philosophy of history and for the ways in which it preempted Christian mental energies for a couple of decades. If successful (or even to the degree that it has already been successful), it portends changes deeper than those effected by the Reformation of the sixteenth century or by the relation of the Church to the thought of the Renaissance or the Enlightenment. One would have to go back to the first Christian centuries, when the men of faith appropriated Greek modes of thinking, to produce the creeds or to the twelfth century when they took from the hands of the hated Turk the "pantheist" thought of Aristotle and helped forge the Catholic synthesis to find precedent for such a radical overhaul of the faith. If so, exploration of this endeavor must rank among the major searches for scripts for the future in Christian history or in the world of our time.

The roots of the new endeavor go back to nineteenth-century Catholic modernism and Protestant liberalism. Both were developmental, evolutionary, progressivistic, optimistic. Both affirmed the world and saw it in continuity with a creator God. Sometimes, as in the case of Frederick Denison Maurice in England, it led to Christian Socialist efforts to remake the social world. At other times, as in the case of the German disciples of Albrecht Ritschl, it led to a kind of bourgeois German embrace of the world as is. In the United States it could blend with a non-Marxian kind of social thought to issue forth in the Social Gospel. In Catholicism it was condemned for its flirtation with heresy, Protestantism, and worldly thought.

The replies to the liberal thought came largely from within the churches; to the contribution of that counterattack we shall return later. Our attempt to locate the roots of the worldly theology move on next to the prophet who inspired so much of the postwar thought, Dietrich Bonhoeffer.[28] He spoke of the *Mündigkeit* of the world, its coming of age; of a religionless Christianity as a future possibility; of a kind of godless man as normative in the human future. He drew on the thought of pioneers like Friedrich Gogarten, who wished to see the desacralizing of the world as a positive good.

This form of thought gained support in Western European (particularly Dutch) Catholicism and in Protestant circles in England and America. American Roman Catholicism more recently devoted itself to the worldly theology.

By now a whole generation of theologians has written important and well-received books in this genre: Paul van Buren, Cornelius van Peursen, Arend van Leeuwen, the durable Bishop John Robinson and the earlier Bishop James Pike, Harvey Cox, Ronald Gregor Smith—these are only a few.[29] For some years the most popular term in the title of theological works was the multipurpose word "secular." We heard of secular churches, secular congregations, secular faith, secular Christianity, secular cities, the secular age. (I am using worldly = secular here, waiting for a moment to define the term and its opposite number, religious.) One cannot accuse these thinkers of failing to try to communicate or their public for failing to respond; some of their books were best-sellers.

Few of these authors are uncritically devoted to the world-oriented or secular theology as they were some years ago. From some points of view, it is now possible to gain a measure of objective distance on the Secular Canon, and the alternative temptation not to treat it as a potent force but as a dead horse/straw man is present. Yet much energy is devoted to it and it has reached into many aspects of the daily life of Christians, for better and for worse. At least, one cannot picture early regress behind the terms of this school of thought, and effort devoted to it may help make our case for it as the most ambitious of the quests for a usable future in recent Christian thought.

For the word "worldly" one must not read simply that element of Biblical thought which sees the world as the demonic or human personification of all that resists the purposes of God ("Love not the world, neither the things that are in the world"[30]). Rather, world represents the whole created order, the world of effects, nature and history treated as neutrally as possible. It stands in opposition to all theologies which locate the drama of creation, rescue, and fulfillment as occurring "out there" in some transcendental, supernatural, or otherworldly realm.

Thus the term "secular" also took on rather neutral connotations. In Christian history it has meant something so mild as the mere removal of ecclesiastical properties and lands to lay or public control or the exposed clergy as opposed to the cloistered "regular" religious. Later it came to mean the mundane world, the world not marked and measured by otherworldly or supernatural influences, an autonomous, desacralized world: one which stands on its own, which rounds itself out, which is a complete story in itself. In its most dramatic and problematic form (and the one use that the positive theologians wanted to avoid) it has meant as "secularism" a thought-out, closed, intact and integral, in no sense neutral order in which thought of the divine is not allowed to intrude.

David Martin[31] and others have shown that the term "secular" is almost never used neutrally and cannot, without extensive explanation, be used unambiguously. Most users bring to it some tendentious and even hidden metaphysical commitment. The rationalists see secular development to be inevitable as reason spreads: the secular is the reasonable, post-theological realm. The Marxists find that it will hold sway when the death of God is celebrated and man and his social processes are free to develop. The existentialists expect the secular world to be revealed when all come to recognize the absurdity of a disordered universe in which men must act anyhow. Still others work with the this-worldly/otherworldly distinction in isolation, unmindful of the problem that some Eastern religions have never been otherworldly yet they are anything but secular by Western definition. The word comes burdened with hazards and potential confusions, but it has located itself in the Christian vocabulary and through it, with new connotations, in the public realm. Men are learning to live with it, to take some care in using it, and to explain themselves.

At the center of the worldly theology is a picture of man in the world: man as a practical, problem-solving, controlling being who is less and less preoccupied with questions about ultimates and about the meaning of the universe. He is the man who is supposed to have been emerging in the West, the man who lives with the knowledge—to use Eric Hoffer's devastating phrase[32]—that God and the priests had seemingly become somehow superfluous yet the world kept going on anyhow. In its minimal definition, "secular" was thus seen merely as man moving on apart from ultimates. Or, maximally, he was seen as having become sure of himself as the killer of the gods and the free person apart from ultimate reference.

Christian thinkers did not, of course, adopt the merely or utterly secular definitions; they were not content with minimal or maximal pictures of worldliness. They controlled the terms with certain concepts from the Christian tradition. They were diffident about talking about God, but they were preoccupied with Jesus Christ (as the man for others) and, in new ways, with the Church. Theirs was the major attempt of our time to search for a usable future that could be applicable to the whole world out of the resources of the Western church.

From theological centers this thought moved out through seminarians, clergy, college students, and informed laity into ever-widening circles. When it reached the public in its most extreme form, as the American Protestant death of God movement, it occasioned much surprise: how could theologians be speaking in such terms and continuing to call themselves theologians? While that movement was restricted to a few persons and was a product in part of mass media of communications, it was an indicator of the depth of durable problems in appropriating the Christian past.

Now, before criticism, for some good words. The worldly trend in theology was responsive to people's needs: it wanted to do justice to a new kind of consciousness. If people did not any longer live in a world of angels and demons, of destinies determined "out there," was it necessary for them to acquire such a world in order to respond to Jesus' call for discipleship? Had he and the apostles not tried to call people out of a world of superstitions, religions, demons, and elemental spirits? Why, asked Paul, should people be thrown back into it?[33]

The new theology was responsible to the Church, if not in conventional ways. That is, while not all its advocates were content with many of the inherited forms of the Church, few of them envisioned a future of religion as being what man does with his solitariness. Most of them taught in seminaries, trained ministers, sought new forms of serving, identified with certain tendencies in the Church. In short, they were churchly but in no sense churchy: they rarely cared about ecclesiastical politics or policies, rubrics or rituals, millinery or prestige.

The secular theologians rather self-consciously tried to pick up momentum from Biblical thought for liberation from static concepts. Their symbols, metaphors, and images were drawn from the Bible. Many of them, in the path of Gogarten, declared (perhaps with a provincial sense) that the momentum of secularization was distinctively Western and drawn from the Bible, where men were to defatalize history and desacralize politics. A study of world religion indicates that such a claim has to be qualified, but the motives behind it reveal the Biblical interests of the thinkers.

They detected a change of mood in the Christian people who most seemed swept up in the service of Christ and men, and they wanted to heighten and enhance it. Instead of narcissistic, crabby,

cribbed defenders of the sanctuary and its traditions, they advocated the development of people who would utter their praise in
the streets, by action as well as by words. They tried and to some
degree succeeded in altering the direction of the Church.

This theology was in almost every instance ethically oriented,
and this not in a late Jansenist or corrupt Puritan form, full of
moralism. Instead, it spoke of a new morality that was oriented
to situations of human need and marked only by the norm of
Christian love. Such an attitude permitted alliance with other
agencies and forces, with people who may not be Christian but
who shared some common goals.

The note of world affirmation was a welcome contrast to so
much of the limp, distanced rejection of the earth and of human
achievement. A note of celebration and joy which had been miss-
ing from many a sanctuary marked its high years. The Sabbath
was not here a withdrawal from the created world but rather a
mark of embrace. For its exorcism, its idol-toppling, demon-purg-
ing, god-killing, it has to be measured as a prophetic protestant
movement. For its devotion to the figure of Jesus it has to be
reckoned with in conventional Christian circles. As a sign of life
in an otherwise inert theological camp it deserved attention. Every
five hundred years or so, one might argue, Christian thought
ought to be able to tolerate a revision, especially if it is directed
to locating properly the scandal of the faith in relation to the
Lordship of Christ and not to the adoption of a particular
thought-world or form of piety or churchmanship. Here was the
courage to change direction, to admit past failures, to engage in
strategic retreat—indeed, to attempt to end the pathetic retreat
from an ever-encroaching secular world. It provided a manual of
arms for countless people.

Any critical word, then, is spoken with regret for the shortcoming of the movement in its prime and with hope for more impetus
in its afterlife.

In what way was this worldly theology a search for a usable
future? To locate it among such quests may seem a bit surprising,
since many advocates and critics saw it as a "now"-theology, a
reportorial impulse at its base. It was often accused of presentism

because it found so much in the past to be useless. As William Hamilton made clear,[34] it was hard for the radical theologians to pick up the Bible, to pray, to go to church, for these practices which had once been meaningful were no longer honest to the contemporary. He was reporting as an autobiographical artist; so were his colleagues. They rejected much past and affirmed much in the present: shall we let it go at that?

A second glance reveals, however, that a consistent if sometimes hidden obsession with the future marked the writings of the whole school. Once again, they spoke in Utopian terms of the new creation as metropolis,[35] of a coming secular city as a kind of new Kingdom of God. Here were scenarios or scripts, possible futures: despite the reportorial guise, all of the spokesmen made clear that the fulfillment or realization had not yet come.

When Eberhard Bethge, the recipient of Bonhoeffer's seminal prison letters and the martyred theologian's editor and biographer, visited the United States an unimpressed university student asked him one night, "How could Bonhoeffer be so dumb as to speak of the world as having come of age? With Nazi guards and signs of Valhalla and Wotan and Christian myth all around him, how could he speak of a post-religious stage?" Bethge answered in effect: "Do you think Bonhoeffer was reporting? He was prophesying. For him, the powers had been defeated, Hitler had been conquered by Christ, and the world had come of age and reached its maturity." (The translation, "world come of age," is a bit misleading in its tense.) Most of the secular theologians have echoed this correction: what they did took on the mode of reporting on man and society. Only a second glance revealed that they were prophesying, arguing from tendency, or writing "as ifs" about the future: secular man and the secular world were not on schedule, not fully present.

Now it appears that the worldly theology has to be seen as a philosophy of history. This sentence is written not to condemn it but to place it. In Arthur Danto's careful distinction, it is a substantive (as opposed to an analytical) philosophy of history.[36] It knows the substance, the outcome, the meaning of the central plot. It deals with the future as if it had already occurred. Man had not come of age, nor had the world; they had not moved into post-religiousness. Bonhoeffer "knew" that they were on the way to such a stage and was quite confident that they would reach it. The analytical historian asks, "How do you know?" He has to wait and see.

The secular theologian is then confronted with many problems. If he contends that he is a present-minded person, merely reporting on what has come about, he has to certify his claims by pointing to the disappearance of religious men and societies (or at least to their near disappearance). This would be most difficult to do in a roomful of sociologists, historians, or politicians. If he is dealing with the future, he must certify on what basis. Has he received a revelation? Is he involved in metaphysical speculation? In either case, he is no longer secular by his own definition, which ruled out revelation, metaphysic, myth, or religious interpretation. If he says he is predicting or prophesying on the basis of trends, his whole effort has to be reread, for he has created a different impression.

If he is most modest and careful, he will probably agree that his has been a prophecy in the form of an imaginative projection. He is not a soothsayer but a seer, not a witch doctor but an artist who discerns the inner meaning of things before others are able to. He somehow has perceived that man and society at the end of the story will be revealed to have been essentially godless or religionless and that only when this secular character was finally revealed and had become triumphant did this inner nature of man become established.

As an imaginative projection it was also a call to action: come, participate in the unfolding of this being, in his liberation from the trammels of vestigial religion! People were invited to engage in a mopping-up operation.

What was seldom noted was how presecular this mode of thinking is unless it is seen purely as a game, a fiction, a writing of an alternative script among many possible scenarios. For it was based on some grand-style Comtean analyses of the human past and future, analyses which then were claimed to be "positivist" but now over a century later are regarded as systematically religious.

Virtually all the secular theologians saw the development of man through some Comtean stages, paralleling the nineteenth-century thinkers' picture of the movement from theological through metaphysical to positive stages. Harvey Cox could see the movement from tribe through town to city; Arend van Leeuwen spoke of the move from ontocratic to technocratic stages; others coined terms to match these.[37] Historically there need be nothing wrong with these analyses, though most historians are uneasy about such sweeping generalizations and would argue with the universal implications of these Westernized observations.

The argument, rather, centers on another point: how do they know that the last Comtean stage is the final one, in which the fulfillment and meaning of history are to be unfolded? If man has progressed through two or three stages, why not through three or four—or seventeen? This is a young world, with all kinds of opportunities for new happenings and surprises. The secular theology knew too much about emerging man; it did not ask what rough beast slouches to Bethlehem to be born—what new religious or spiritual forces, liberating or oppressing, are emerging in this fertile period, to say nothing of those that might still be ahead. It is in the unquestioned assumption about the fulfilled stage of secular man and secular society that this theology transgressed its own ground rules and appears unimaginative and timid from one point of view (as it underestimates future possibilities) or too arrogant (as it takes for granted its vision of the future without questioning it).

Better luck next time? If indeed the worldly or secular theology goes down with this built-in deficiency, it is possible to ask some questions about what can be learned from the venture. Some of the criticisms have an emotional tinge. There is the danger that reckless scripts for the future, if presented as reportage or inevitable fulfillments, can lead to frustration and reaction. The theologians write manuals of arms for the believers, and by the time the lay people begin to get their marching orders, the theologians have gone off in a different direction. How much confidence should the faithful have in leaders so moved by mood and cultural shift that they can create optimistic secular theologies and then, a few fires and a few assassinations and one small war later, call it all off and begin at the beginning? Some found it reasonable to ask whether they would not have been better off all along with the fundamentalists, who were out of things before, during, and after this theological revolution. Rather have one confusion than three. The conservatives often did try to exploit the sense of change, though their credentials were weak, for they had displayed little creative energy in meeting any of the change.

One of the legacies of the radical or new theology was its sense of impoverishment. The wry British critics accused its spokesmen of having written excellent cookbooks after having burned down the kitchen. Others used the picture of their having jettisoned the tools needed to repair a leaky ship. From another point of view, however, the movement had helped put theology on a fresh and chastened basis. Many of the theologians learned that in making the move from seminaries to the larger culture, secular people were more secular than they had envisioned ("just atoms and molecules and *that's it!*") and religious people were religious in more varied ways than they had remembered.

More substantively, this major modern search for a usable future on Christian terms has to be faulted on both anthropological and theological grounds. Anthropology first: did it use a sufficiently broad model of man? While its spokesmen had every right to posit a kind of sunny, happy, carefree, agnostic and essential or fulfilled man and to see all societal trends as pointing to his emergence, were they performing a service by screening out so many countervailing factors and conflicting evidences?

The sociologists and the historians were at a loss to know where the theologians were deriving their model for man. From Sweden? Perhaps: Sweden gives evidence of making a transition from a religious culture to one in which few people do more than the barest nominal service to religious reminiscence (in baptism, confirmation, marriage, and burial) and who seem to be devising mores and morals largely independent of historic religious ones. So some say. Did they draw it from California or Japan, areas of rapid industrial, technological, and academic growth—and the scenes of the emergence or recovery of hundreds of astonishing kinds of religious movements? Is it fair to extrapolate from the working-hours' life of healthy Western academic and technological men and assume that all history will follow the Western course?

While the theologians were busy, the sociologists (like Thomas Luckmann, David Martin, Ernest Gellner, J. Milton Yinger, and Gerhard Lenski) [38] were charting just as profound sea changes. But they were diffident about speaking concerning essential or fulfilled man and society. They were less sure about where he was going and were more concerned to point out that what men were seeing was radical change—whether secularization was the best word for this was questionable. Luckmann spoke of a transformation of symbols in industrial society. Institutional religion is radically assaulted and altered—there seems to be no question about that. Man's sacred cosmos and his world view, with an almost inevitable theological dimension, are also altered, but they usually provide for a relocation or a reformulation of religious impulses. Gellner saw the religion which had helped society pass over a hump of transition remaining as a kind of moraine on the societal landscape for an indefinite period. J. Milton Yinger spoke not of secularization but of radical religious change under symbols of nonchange. These pictures are less glamorous but more faithful to things as they now are.

These men also wrote their scenario for the future. In effect, men like Gellner and Yinger at least tell their readers, societies seem to be developing relatively stable and necessary lay, civil, or societal religions. The secular theologians would disagree with such scenarios, regarding these folk religions as problematic from a normative Christian point of view. The social analysts counter: what is the basis of your right to speak of something as being normative? Can you cite it without cheating on the rules of your own "secular" game—that is, without opening the door to revelation, myth, or metaphysics?

Theologians do their work on an anthropological base. They have to talk about man. For some years they chose to minimize his prolific and protean religious tendencies and to speak of religious change in the all-inclusive category of secularization. Taking little responsibility for addressing his religious side, they saw him making his way to horoscope readers, psychedelic drug priests, and the caretakers of folk religion.

The theological questions of this search concern us less directly at this point. One might fault the thinkers for choosing the easy part of the theological task. They devoted themselves to Jesus, arguing that it was difficult for the Church to see him as fully human and worldly. But that lesson is more easily learned than the harder one: what did he mean when he spoke of one who sent him? It was easy to hear him say, "He who has seen me has seen the Father." It is more difficult to make theological sense today of his "He who believes in me, believes not in me but in him who sent me."[39] It is easy to speak of his thisworldliness; it is harder to speak of his unmistakable otherness.[40]

From the point of view of Protestant theology, one must question whether Jesus-without-God did not receive too high a status among the secular Christians. They often spoke in ultimate terms of his call, his demand, his promise. In classic Protestant terms, so to repair to a man among men is to engage in idolatry. Must he not be transparent to something or someone else, wherein ultimate commitment can be more properly grounded? These questions were rarely faced in the world-oriented theology, eager as it was to shun "God-talk" and to concentrate on the human figure of Jesus and the believing community. For the theologians were asking for more than a humanism with a reminiscence of Jesus. Or if they were asking for only that, why Jesus and not Jefferson, who is more immediately accessible as an author and guarantor of freedom?

Eventually the theological shortcomings of the movement caught up with it, and the thinkers are working once again on a meaningful word about God or some other way of speaking about the reality to which Jesus pointed. The world? In Albert Schweitzer's terms, "The world affirms itself." It does not seem to need the aid of seminarians and theologues. The secular theologians were neither merely nor utterly secular: they always smuggled in

highly evocative Christian symbols. This is what made them theologians. Today we are in the situation later men were in, in relation to a nineteenth-century school: "from them we have
learned much, but now have to unlearn more."

4

The Present's Twofold Sign

The world-oriented theology of the postwar period, culminating in the new Protestant and Catholic theology of the early 1960s, was marked by a single sign: it foresaw a growing rationality in the world and saw the convergence between its fulfillment and the Kingdom of God. In this, it shared the single-mindedness of the classic Utopias. In the process, it temporarily replaced some of the dystopias which had marked the period between the two World Wars in Europe. Dystopia or Armageddon is marked by the sign of a growing absurdity and sense of meaninglessness. It foresees man moving to destruction.

The creative quest for a usable future, unless it is willing to repeat the errors of both the optimistic and pessimistic theologies, with their eventual consequence—the disillusionment of the illusioned or the immobilizing of the depressed—will have to incorporate both extremes of human existence. Such a double vision will lack some of the neatness and drama of the single-minded versions. Those who work with it may seem less audacious than are the writers of positive or negative scenarios. They may also be more faithful to the character of history, the complex dimensions of human existence, and the needs of people willing to put up with complexity.

When one reads the plays from the Theater of the Absurd he finds much in them to corroborate his observations about the apparent pointlessness of human existence; but they do not prepare him to account for the chinks of affirmation in the gloom, for the marks of grace and the signals and occasions for eucharist. When one reads the optimistic theology of the recent past, with its simple affirmation of new frontiers and great societies and updated churches, he feels as distant as he does from the world of Akhnaton or Dionysius the Areopagite: can men so recently as that have seen such a clear linear picture of human fulfillment?

Translate the terms to the extremes of personal development: did the controlled definition of the secular do justice to the real godless condition of man? Did the self-assured picture of the disappearance of religion square with the picture of the real world which a reporter or analyst would bring from a survey of the scene? These questions relate to some throwaway lines in the previous chapter and must be enlarged upon as the first positive step in setting forth a view of usable futures.

Suppose one were to argue the opposite of what world-oriented theology did. We have seen it to be a substantive philosophy of history marked by a disguised metaphysics of progress. It can be faulted for having too clear and sure an image of what man at the end of history (or in his essence) really is: godless, post-religious, simply worldly. The opposite vision would argue that man, society, and the world are through and through religious. One can resurrect the classic picture of *homo religiosus,* the man with such deep roots in human history.

The argument for religious man begins with the empirical situation. Until recently most men most places have appeared to be religious. That is, they set out to relate to an unseen world behind this visible world or they tried to come to terms with the sacral and the divine in the middle of this world. To that end primitive men set out to appease the gods. Many of the traces of early man can be related to religion. Then humans went through a long stage of amazingly rich religious inventiveness. The great religions were born within a millennium of each other and came from their birthplace in Asia to influence and even dominate later Asia and Europe. Meanwhile, cultural anthropologists for scores of years have encountered new isolated primitive men, all of whom have some sense of the sacred.

The presence of secular man in the period since the Renaissance and the Enlightenment then has to be explained away. He is a temporary aberration, one beguiled by his own achievements into forgetting his source and goal in the divine realm. One day there will be a new awakening. Or he can be seen as an extremely rare phenomenon, the occasional and offbeat alienated person at the edges of society—or a member of a rare elite that gathers in academia and in other eccentric settings. As such, he is a less than whole man, one whose deviations have to be explained pathologically. But since there are so many like him and they fill so many personality stereotypes some other explanation must be found.

The third approach designates the secular man as a religious person in strange plumage. He is really religious but does not know it. He only apparently lacks ultimate concern. Our society makes it possible for him to forget about ultimate issues and to screen out all references to his own impending death and the need to come to terms with his destiny. The distractions of the world keep him from serious reflection on the spiritual. The shortcomings of religious institutions may have given him good reason for isolating himself from them and for avoiding conventional worship. But in his heart of hearts and soul of souls there is a divine spark burning, one which can be ignited some night when he is afraid after the diagnosis of a malignancy or in crisis when his wife is on the point of leaving him. Then his true, his religious nature will be manifest!

The third approach goes beyond the empirical situation. One can follow the new kind of godless man around for years, waiting to pounce on him in a clear-cut act of being religious and finding nothing. He can see the man participating in a society that cannot be called officially religious, but our analyst waits: sooner or later its godlessness will vanish and it will rewrite its charter with a metaphysical or revelational cause. Then the case can be made—only it never is.

Those who argue for *homo religiosus* operate with historic definitions of man and his world. For instance, the Christian tradition does not anticipate the godless man. By definition he does not fit in. But, continues John Courtney Murray with a studied sense of naïve irony, "there he is. That is the problem."[41]

Homo religiosus in full-dress form, then, is more the product of a substantive philosophy of history than he is the result of analytical observation. By revelation or by metaphysical calculation one comes to the conclusion that man is essentially religious; though his religion be true or false, he cannot escape being oriented toward some sort of religion. *A priori,* it is decided that the world can never come of age. Man must live out his years under the tutelage of the gods. He must follow a specific form of piety and will see omens, signs, wonders, superstitions, and marks of ultimate concern.

The historian cannot disprove this view of the human future any more than he can that of final and essential secular man. If he points to godless man, his philosopher-of-history friend will enlarge the definition of religion to include the godless. The returns are not all in yet, he continues. Give me time and I may come across secular man and secular society, is his next plea. No luck: his friend knows what man is; he knows the outcome of history. The analytical type is frustrated in the face of both alternatives.

The third course remains open. It focuses on Burckhardt's "one eternal center of all things—man, suffering, striving, doing." In concentration on him, the historian is free of all burden of prediction or prophecy. He needs no intact philosophy of history to encompass man and all men, no elastic set of definitions to prove that man is essentially or finally one thing or another. But this does not rule him out from reporting on and taking part in shaping the story of man.

The historian can see man as Paul Ricoeur sees his world. "The modern world can be viewed under the twofold sign of a growing rationality along with a growing absurdity."[42] Neither trend is static. The man of the past could not begin to bring reason into control as can the man of the computer age. The man of the past rarely envisioned the meaninglessness as have recent artists or dramatists. In no previous century could men face the physical needs of all men and realistically expect to meet them and at the same time hold the weapons which could destroy all men.

Ricoeur's twofold sign can be translated into many realms. Thus a historian could argue that man, men, and societies today are observable under the twofold sign of a growing secularity and a growing religiousness. (Needless to say, in this parallelism I am not equating secularity with rationality and religiousness with absurdity, but only pointing to two poles of existence.)

Such a twofold vision has two great assets. On the one hand, it is a verifiable and sensible interpretation of the world of effects. Men have striven to be increasingly religious and in some ways are observably so, though their religions undergo fantastic transformations and change. And men have chosen to live in a basically desacralized cosmos, purged of deity and the divine: this is also demonstrable. In order to tell the story of the past, including the immediate past, it is not necessary to rule out one whole set of signs or one whole kind of evidences.

The other asset lies in the contribution of this view to the task of making imaginative projections about the future. It provides for a wider and deeper range of models and, in terms of the previous chapter, allows for a richer anthropological archetype. While less is ventured, more can be gained. There is no possibility of the frustration caused by failed Utopias or of the passivity or terror caused by the depiction of Armageddons. In these respects, such a twofold vision contributes to the historian's task, for he has no ideological commitment which leads him to screen out one kind of evidence. It liberates him for action.

To enlarge upon this twofold picture of man, I shall revert to the writings of a dialectical thinker whose thought can never be fashionable to Utopians or Armageddonites, Paul Tillich. In an autobiographical work written at mid-career he told of some precommitments he brought to his work. Strophe by strophe his portrait can be of help in enlarging on Ricoeur's theme.[43]

First, Tillich's view of life "includes a consciousness of the corruption of existence." It is possible to resist speculation on how this came to be and even whether it shall always be so. One needs no ontological or structural basis for this in the universe of effects and meaning. So far, says the analyst, this is how things are; this can be observed. People die. The righteous suffer. Babies are neglected and killed. Hunger strikes the innocent. War endures. Hatred seems to counter love. Men destroy nature and pollute creation. The concentration camp is a mark of the current century. One could extend the list only at the risk of continuing to be obvious and banal. But he will be citing the facts which optimistic philosophies of history have to overlook or hurry past. Secular theologians dismissed those who cited these facts as being gloomy existentialists; there had been no room for the tragic sense.

The analyst who begins with this vision can say that if history turns out otherwise, against overwhelming odds, he will not be off the mark, for he has not ruled out any possibility. The Christian may have as an aspect of his faith the final overcoming of this corruption in existence, but such finality does not belong to history as it is now lived. For all practical purposes, he can go on assuming that the world will remain tainted by a corruption that affects all men and things. This does not mean that he has to celebrate Sisyphus and see life as the pointless pushing of a burden up a hill, only to see the need to start again. One can make all kinds of choices and interpretations in the face of and in spite of the corruption of existence.

Second, this view includes "a repudiation of every kind of social Utopia (including the metaphysics of progressivism)." Tillich was fighting one strand of reformed Christianity which he could never understand. He ran counter to a durable motif in Catholic modernism and Protestant liberalism, and seemed to deny one element in the American creed. Yet reflective Americans have been able to see that their frequently stated belief in progress is grounded more in hope than in the empirical reality. A nation that preempted its soil by committing virtual genocide against the people who were there earlier and that has held on to its wealth by enslaving a black minority and suppressing them after emancipation has come to see the contradictory underside of its optimistic life. Now that it is reaping the benefits of its earlier imperial policies in reaction to inflexible Cold War policies, it is coming to see that in the eyes of the world the picture of American innocence is not transportable.

The repudiation of social Utopias and the metaphysics of progress that survived to color even the recent theology is not to be undertaken in such a way that the benefits of actions carried on under their sway are lost. One does not repudiate Utopia in order to engage in self-flagellation or masochism but only to be free to deal with situations as they develop and not by eliminating countertestimony to what is seen.

A third dimension is "an awareness of the irrational and demonic nature of existence." Such a statement may have a mythic cast. It is not necessary to place it in the angelic-demonic setting for the point to come through. Even without mythic reference it is clear. A decade which speaks of the bestiality of the naked ape of African genesis in his path of aggression ought to be open to see the tug and pull between the views of man's reason and his irrationality, between his dream and the demons which haunt him. At least, this dimension makes possible the preparation of the historian's consciousness to be able to live with every kind of ugliness. A colleague, when asked what philosophy he has learned from his study of history, contends only this: "That every folly and every vice that man can conceive of he has undertaken."

Other aspects of Tillich's precommitment are less important here. They include "an appreciation of the mystical element in religion," a point that would not need to be brought up here were it not for the fact that this mystical bent was manifest again in the midst of the secular culture right after the worldly theology had made its point about the secular future. This mystical appreciation adds to the picture a play element: not all that man does must be immediately purposive and grimly productive.

The last element: "a rejection of Puritan legalism in private and corporal life." This has little to do with the theology in question, which was not basically legalistic. At least in relation to the world it was catholic and embracing; its view of the Church was more protestant, Puritan, and rigorous or self-denying.

What is left to work with, one might legitimately ask, if these countertendencies have to be reckoned with? The Utopian is nettled by reference to them. But they can provide a realistic basis for scenario writing among those who can tolerate ambiguity, Luther writes that God carves the rotten wood and rides the lame horse. But, he implies, God carves, God rides. The raw material of which the human future is to be made includes rotten wood and lame horses, but it does not necessarily include the avoidance of carving and riding.

Those who see in history something of what Tillich posits there will find it impossible to identify with the main line of recent theology on simple secular lines. The Secular City did turn out to be Camelot; the new creation which was metropolis turned out to be an ungovernable and is now a burning entity. Secular man is no longer in control; for a time he was even seen trailing off behind yogis and gurus. Fortunately, most of the originators of this school of thought have also redrafted their charts and revised their simplistic views of human tendency. They are working with richer anthropological models, to the benefit of theology.

The twofold vision of human growth relates to the historian's "wait and see" attitude. With Nietzsche he believes that "man is an indeterminate being." He is his praxis, his project; he becomes what his values commit him to. He is "multivalented," in one sociologist's terms;[44] he is a product in part of his culture, and not all cultural possibilities have yet unfolded.

When the Christian comes along to say that this view is not sufficient, he usually supplies elements based upon Scriptural revelation. Man is a sinner. Man is saved. These may well be true, but they do not add to the empirical framework, for the Christian tradition also says that these dimensions of humanity will be revealed in man, depending upon his faith, his hope, his love. He remains an indeterminate being, and the societal future is also undecided inside history.

This argument will be misunderstood if it is taken to mean that because the optimistic world-oriented theologies stressed the godless future it is now necessary to compensate and stress the religious future. In that case, "indeterminacy" would be a category introduced for the biding of time or as an opening wedge for a hidden metaphysic about *homo religiosus*. The interest, rather, is reportorial, designed to build in anticipation for the extremes of godless and religious man. The secular theology hedged and controlled its picture of human secularity: somehow atoms-and-molecules-that's-all-there-is man was expected to respond to symbols dealing with the Lordship of Christ, the Easter faith, the pilgrim Church. Is such a man secular? The twofold view allows everything to be what it is.

Some may question whether this "twofold view" is really a view or vision at all. Is it not too timid, too modest, too uninspiring to serve as a motor for human action? Is not history made by seers who exaggerate, distort, creatively mislead? The point is this: the Christian vision of history allows for exaggeration of both tendencies in man and society. On one hand, it can stare at the depths of the human reality without blinking; on the other, it hopes "beyond hope," as it were, knowing that the final victory belongs to God as the power of the future and to Christ as the one who has removed "the deadliness of death." Similarly, the twofold view of man as a secular and as a religious being allows for frank empirical assessment as well as truly unlimited possibility.

This means that we do not need to rub our hands in glee when we find the soft underbelly of religiousness behind the stiff back of the secular beast. On the contrary, religious man can be as great a problem to faith as secular man could ever be. This at least was well established by Karl Barth and Dietrich Bonhoeffer in their long and frequent polemics against religion:[45] this is where we came in! The man of religious bent is self-preoccupied; his hands and ears are full; he is not likely to be open to a message of judgment or of surprising grace. There is here, then, no interest in finding *homo religiosus* as the beginning of an apology for Christianity but only in finding man as he is and society as it is, to allow for broader and deeper interpretations of destiny.

Since the overwhelming weight of argument in recent years has dealt with the presence of secular man, it is now in place to balance the picture with some portrayals of religious man and society. If the definitions of secular were complex and blurry, this is even more true of religious. Definitions which restrict religion to religious institutions are obviously too narrow. On the other hand, those which denominate all serious dimensions of life "religious" seem too broad to be functional. Provisionally, we can cite some dimensions of religiousness which are necessary only to balance the secular picture.

Religiousness would imply some sort of attempt at relating to meaning or, for many, all the reality there is; to ultimacy. One normally expects this to be enhanced symbolically or ceremonially. Such enhancement can be on through formal institutions of religion, through private ritual, or through formal but unreflective public observance—like marking money with the phrase "In God We Trust." Some sort of sanction (metaphysical, mythical, or their equivalent) will normally be sought for that which is called religious. And, often, the religious will seek a communal expression as a starting point or a bonus: for many, religion involves great numbers of people in pointing to one thing.

In these descriptions one is not confined to formal high religions; but on the other hand, the definition is not so broadened that everything becomes religious, so nothing is. What I have striven for is the obverse to Harvey Cox's understandably well-accepted definition of secularization as "the loosing of the world from religious and quasi-religious understandings of itself, the dispelling of all closed world-views, the breaking of all supernatural myths and sacred symbols."[46]

Where is secular man, then, absent? In the United States, which bears the marks of a secular-religious (or religio-secular) order, one would have to call into question the designation secular for the 97 per cent of the people who respond positively to the poll-takers' question, "Do you believe in God?" It would more certainly rule out the 63 per cent of the people who have affiliated with religious institutions. Even more emphatically he is absent from that 44 per cent of the population which was at religious services during the past week.

The secular theologian is ready with a response: certainly, we all know in our bones that something has happened to man. He does not necessarily mean what his father did when his father asserted belief in God; he does not expect what his father expected when he joined the church; he does not do what his forebears did when he goes to worship. Way down deep he is the product of a new age and a new spirit. To all of these contentions one can only enter a hearty agreement. Further, the theologian, operating from some normative point of view or other, may enter his complaints about the quality of the religion implied in these figures. The definitions of deity are vague. People join institutions out of habit. They can worship in bad faith as well as in faith. Again, agreed. Much of the religious identification may be casual and inauthentic. It is possible, however, to share the theologians' normative judgment and to disagree with them analytically. The reporter must take more seriously the complex of motives for religious response and must bracket his suspicions about genuineness and authenticity.

Beyond the most obvious symbols and institutional ties, religion finds many other locations. The observer finds the citizen at Lincoln Memorial or the Tomb of the Unknown Soldier acting religiously by any historic definition. He sees him participating in rites of passage associated not with Church but with nation. He hears the rhetoric associated with foreign demons and homeland angels, of the God of battles and the punisher of dissenters. He hears advocacy for the ultimate truth of the American Business Creed and sees the absolute devotion to the gods of success. He watches people going through the countless rituals of daily and interpersonal life.

When the conventional and orthodox are not looking he observes secular man scurrying off to buy the morning paper to read his horoscope, or to the newsstand to join the three million citizens who regularly buy horoscope magazines. He listens to late-night television and finds few celebrities able to sign off without eighteen benedictions and a dozen superstitions. He hears of the vogues for seances and spiritual realization, for transcendental meditation and Zen. He begins to wonder where secular man is hiding.

None of these observations are designed to minimize the extent to which people have been able to desert religious institutions or to improvise new modes of life. It is only to point out that even industrialized, affluent, technological societies present ambiguous testimony on man and where he is going. That there is change is obvious; that the change follows predetermined lines is questionable.

The coinage "religio-secular" to characterize the past, the present, and the tendency of American society, is not very fortunate, but we have not heard more elegant alternatives. If persons and the society as such manifest such tendencies, they are in a long tradition, not too different from that of the Greco-Roman world in which Christianity was born. Then, too, a civic religion embraced all but a few dissenters. Then, too, a host of new religions sprang up and flourished at the side of old ones. And then as now people tried to cope with and celebrate naturalistic and scientific views of order. Evidently inside the matrix of a mixed society people are able to improvise endlessly. Over against this picture, today's theology is Protestant: it says not, "Whom you ignorantly worship, him declare I unto you," as Paul had it, but, "Whom you ignorantly worship, him will I kill off, if only I can catch him."

The theologian announces to the culture: your god is dead. The institutions of religion seem irrelevant and insecure. But they have not left a vacuum. New religious forces fill their place.

When these elements are faced in the writing of a scenario dealing with the future of religion, numerous choices are available. Men can use the old scenario, expecting the present religious complex to last. When in doubt, bet on establishment. But such a view is far too conservative in the face of profound societal change.

A second script advises: given man's mixed secular and religious character, men must start from scratch and devise what

Walter Lippmann so long ago called "the religion of the spirit"[47] or what Arnold Toynbee has advocated as a kind of coexistence or blending of the best in world religions. A third course would be to see the past rewritten in the present: the past forms undergo conscious and unconscious, explicit and implicit, transformation.

A full Christian criticism and program would include both Protestant and Catholic elements. The prophetic or protestant aspect says that religiousness can be imprisoning and confining. The world is not yet desacralized and defatalized enough. Man would be more dignified and whole if he could junk his horoscopes and institutional security blankets. The idols have to be smashed and the gods killed. The catholic aspect says that man dare not be abandoned without some point of stability in the midst of change. He also holds a responsibility in culture. He is to construct, to build, to heal, to reconcile, to integrate: it is psychologically intolerable and socially impossible to have everyone and everything off-balance all the time.

In the scenario writing, Christians are given a variety of institutional choices. They can try to keep up appearances, as if Christendom were still alive. They can keep alive some aristocratic sense, like an elite in a wayward world. They can recognize their exilic or diasporal status. In all but the first cases they can help be custodians of the human story.

The protestant-catholic vision seems to imply a Machiavellian or manipulative view of the future. In a sense this is present in the future-game: when man reveals too strongly religious tendencies and begins to become secure and caught up in himself, his spiritual life, his personal salvation, the protesting blast scorns his solemn assemblies and his incense or preening scrupulosity. When he appears to be unreflectively or inauthentically secular, he can be confronted by the potential in spiritual resources and can be faced with riddles of human existence which he may be overlooking.

The citation of the evidences of ongoing human religiousness alongside the secular scope has done nothing at all to advance the substance of theology, or at least of its central subject. That is, man's durable religiousness does not present any new evidence for the existence of God. By the ground rules of theological inquiry such evidence could not conceivably be offered. For as evidence is now reckoned, one would have to wheel out a deity for demonstration and verification. Yet if something could be wheeled out, it could not be God.

Similarly, the anthropological discussion has done nothing directly in the line of presenting evidence against the existence of God. William Hamilton put it well when he said, "We are not talking about the absence of the experience of God, but about the experience of the absence of God."[48] But in so doing he did not escape the circle of immanence. He did not find it possible to carry report from some transcendent, metaphysical realm where the final answers could be presumed to be. He did not escape nor try to escape that circle in which evangelist Billy Graham operated when he said, "I know that God is alive. I talked to him this morning." What Graham and Hamilton, from opposite perspectives, have succeeded in doing is to enrich our anthropological model. They have stretched the poles between which theological talk goes on. The evidence to this point is clear: man and society remain indeterminate. The outcomes are not yet available.

So far, it is apparent that when religion is suppressed or when it withers in one form it bobs up somewhere else. Is man, then, secular or religious? A put-off answer can be, "Yes." He will be defined in his praxis, his values, his quest. "It does not yet appear what we shall be."

Near the end of Leslie Dewart's famous book on *The Future of Belief*[49] he set forth a program that strikes the reader as being possessed of more imagination than either the secular theology or the advocates of *homo religiosus* had to offer. Dewart advised against placing *a priori* limits on the levels to which human consciousness conceivably could rise. It may be possible to conceive of God in the future in better or nobler ways than in the past. (I would prefer to say: in ways as appropriate to a new day as past conceptions were in the old.)

This is not the point to examine the full theological implications of Dewart's argument. What matters now, instead, is the anthropological argument. If I were to enlarge upon its context, it would read something like this:

What is so good about secular man? So long as people romanticize the secular and the world, they look good. They represent the realm of human freedom and inquiry. Secular man is not haunted nor disturbed by the riddle and mystery of existence. He takes life as it comes, does not ask too many questions, and is a productive and apparently fulfilled person. The problem is, the theologians have tipped their hands by calling for a very particular kind of secular man. Their kind has been shaped by Christian influences, or coincidentally (as in the case of Albert Camus, an early hero of the worldly theology) he addresses himself to Christian themes. He rages against the injustice of the gods but wants to carry on respectful dialogue with Christians. Like Roger Garaudy, to take another instance, he is a new-style Marxist who wants conversation with Christians.[50]

These are contrived and cozy models for secularity so far as Christians are concerned. They are more attractive than the secular people who have no curiosity about anything evoked by Biblical symbolism or Christian reminiscence. Indeed, the theologian who has venerated secular man could quite possibly find that he would not want to spend a dinner hour with him: he could turn out to be sterile, devoid of a sense of depth and mystery, compulsive about his leisure and pleasure, and grim about the world of production—in short, the kind of being against whom the hippies had to carry on revolt in the name of "soul."

On the other hand, what is so good about *homo religiosus?* His defenders are also forced to defend a kind of half-man, whose maturity—in Bonhoeffer's familiar interpretation—has been thwarted because he is constantly being thrown back into a kind of spiritual adolescence. He grows past bizarre explanations of reality based on reference to a god who fills in the gap of human ignorance. Then he is told that such a god must be reintroduced to round out the picture of reality—that he will somehow be better off for such a reintroduction! Will the religious man be a better servant of the human city, preoccupied as he must be with the question, "How am I doing, God?"

In the face of these alternatives, Dewart asks for the development of a new kind of human consciousness not marked by either of these obsolete pictures. A critic once said of the thought of Ernst Troeltsch: it is frustrating to be told in advance what one is going to be permitted to believe. In the face of false alternatives one is tempted to say: it is defeating to be told in advance what man and society are going to be allowed to become.

A preferable alternative seems to be the religio-secular model of indeterminacy, open to infinite transformations and toward the development of new kinds of consciousness. Such consciousness would belong to people who would not have escaped history, but who could face it with fresh resources.

5

Toward a Future with Hope

The search for an approach to the future is motivated by quests for meaning and opportunities to serve. If the Christian community is looking for a new direction, it should be motivated by concern for people and not simply with revision of schools of theology. But in that community today, theology has achieved a new position, and revisionism has an eventual effect on the daily life of Christian people. For that reason it is a worthwhile task to trace the trend of Christian thought after criticism of secular theology began.

This worldly theology turned out to be monodimensional: it was too confident about the direction of human history and too sure of the meaning of the process of secularization. Further, it was colored by an optimism which, when frustrated, leads to people's loss of confidence in Christian leadership and loss of motivation for action. In place of this simplistic view of history we have argued for an approach which retains the ambiguity of history and yet which motivates action and prevents paralysis.

Religious thought has been devoted most recently to a kind of theology which can do justice to the complex human situation and still pick up some of the inspiring notes from the Christian thought of the decades preceding it.

The hunger for such a motif has led many to seek and point to "the theology of hope" as an all-purpose answer. In part the advocacy of such an inclusive theology has satisfied those who seek novelty for its own sake, those who need to classify everything and give passion to the newest. In that case, the Christian community would have to envision a generation of effort put into a single movement. People would have to join up for a cause; a new establishment in theology would ostracize those who happen to have other concerns and refine the subtler points of the new school. Before Protestant and Catholic theologians take such a turn, it may be well to ask how the churches have come to such a moment and whether the new movement, if it is to become one, can bear all the weight it would have to as a motor for Christian action in the decades ahead.

Those who have had little to do with the history of theology can best locate the current call against the background of a brief recall of earlier twentieth-century thought. I shall trace Protestant directions; for a number of reasons, Roman Catholicism had an isolated development until Vatican Council II. Since that time, its theologians have picked up where they left off threescore years ago when Modernism was condemned; today Protestant and Catholic thought parallel each other.

At the end of the eighteenth century, after the period of Enlightenment and Aufklärung, a Christian in Europe could well have prophesied the death of theology, of the Church, of God. In France, a generation had concentrated on "crushing the infamy" that was the Church and supplanting its thought with a complete alternative synthesis. Yet the nineteenth century saw a rebirth of Protestant thought and an attempt on the part of Catholic thinkers to relate the themes of faith to an emerging world view. Since their probing was cut off when Modernism was condemned, it is more useful to turn to the Protestant career in the nation where modern theology has received most attention.

In Germany, it would have been hard to foresee a new charter for theology at the beginning of the nineteenth century. Then came Friedrich Schleiermacher, who by concentrating on the experiencing subject was among those who established a base for doing theology. Throughout the nineteenth century themes from Schleiermacher were enhanced and enlarged. At the same time, other theologians, drawing on inspiration from the Hegelians and the neo-Kantians, experimented and engaged in innovation. By the end of the century what we now call liberal theology was quite well established.

The liberal theology stressed continuities between supernature and nature, faith and reason, nature and grace, the God-man Jesus and all men, the Kingdom of God and the community of men. As its critics later were to point out, this school of thought was optimistic, progressivistic, and ordinarily uncritical of the trend of modern bourgeois life. By the beginning of World War I this upbeat, developmental, and positive school of thought pervaded the German universities and found analogies in Anglican modernism, Roman Catholic modernism, and the American New Theology and Social Gospel.

The onset of World War I seemed to many to represent the death of nineteenth-century humanism, bourgeois life, and a Christian civilization. New pessimistic and critical styles of thought began to emerge, more or less along the lines that were later to be called existentialist. Symbolic of the change in Christian circles will always be the name of the new orthodox theologian of crisis, Karl Barth. In the dark of that night, he was later to say, he reached for something to which to hold: it turned out to be the bell rope. The activity of Barth, signaled by his dialectical commentary on Paul's Letter to the Romans, along with that of his colleagues and competitors, was a reaction to liberalism. Bourgeois values came under judgment. Human achievements, especially in relation to the coming Kingdom of God, were devalued. Now the stress was on discontinuity: God was the Wholly Other, there was no point of contact between a redeeming God and an aspiring man in the make-up or achievement of man. The metaphysic of progress was smoked out and then expunged from Christian thought.

This new orthodoxy prevailed, with countless variations, in

European theology until well after World War II. In the United States the reaction to liberalism was somewhat later; most historians date it from the beginning of the 1930s. At that time the coming of the Great American Depression accomplished for Americans what the war had done for Europe: it called into question the values of normalcy and jolted the complacent out of their self-confident sense of progress and achievement. The writings of the native Niebuhr brothers, the translation of the writing of Karl Barth, and the influence of the exiled theologian Paul Tillich were among the shaping forces of the new orthodox, crisis thought, and the new critical realism in the United States. It coexisted with Continental and the less dramatically reactionary British thought through World War II and well into the 1950s.

At this time it might be fruitful to play a Hegelian thesis-antithesis-synthesis game, without treating that game as an all-purpose or inevitable approach to history. If the liberal theology was the thesis and the new orthodox thought was the antithesis, then the worldly theology was a kind of synthesis. Take "worldly" first: I have preferred that term here to secular, for it recaptures a strong theme of the liberal era. This world is the milieu of divine activity; in its emergent process God works out his purpose and here he ushers in his Kingdom; it provides the stuff of theology. Again and again the theologians of the 1960s were accused of resuscitating liberalism, with its optimistic and progressive thought. If they were action-oriented, they were described as repristinators of the old Social Gospel. Some of them rightfully resented these labels, not because they disagreed with the designations so much as because they knew that nothing in history can or should be repeated and because there was significant newness in their own thought. They were unwilling to carry all the burdens and legacies of the older and sometimes superficial liberalism. Yet their own thought did have sources in the interrupted liberalism of a half century and more earlier.

At the same time, most of the secular theologians were also described as drawing on neo-orthodoxy. William Hamilton tried to describe the thought of Harvey Cox as "pop-Barth"; to the degree that this was applicable, the designation seems curious. How could the same man incarnate something of the Social Gospel era and of its successor and repudiator? Yet Cox and the others who drew on Bonhoeffer did have strands of both the progressivistic and the revelational in their systems. When the detailed history of theology in their period is written, no doubt it will be seen that much of the basis for this synthesis goes back to Bonhoeffer, who had studied both under the liberals at Berlin and indirectly under Barth.

What is more, the new orthodoxy was born out of liberalism and had never been able to suppress its themes or its agenda. The two were bone of each other's bone and flesh of each other's flesh. Under all the polemic and exaggeration on the part of advocates of each, there was a common ground on which the secular theology built. But if that world-directed theology was a synthesis, it was short-lived and in a way premature.

The Christian world is moving on from that style of doing theology. When one of the old Hegelians was asked why history does not reach a stasis in a time of synthesis, he remarked that the new development in history will itch and it will have to be scratched. This can be translated to mean in the present instance that the secular theology moved on by the demands of an inner necessity. The best criticisms of the accent came from its earliest advocates, who were eager to revise it just about the time it began to meet wide public acceptance in the churches. At the same time, external circumstances (the deaths of Pope John, President Kennedy, Martin Luther King; the escalation of the war in Vietnam; the ghetto revolts and the breakdown of civil rights integrationism) served as occasions for change in context and mood much as World War I and the Depression had done to earlier schools.

Forget the Hegelian game, now. At this point it should be expected that a call for the post-synthetic theology should be issued. Everybody should now repudiate liberalism, new orthodoxy, and secular theology. On the contrary (and this will come as a surprise to no one who knows historians with their junk shop, accumulating, "can't-throw-anything-away" mentality): it is important to consolidate the gains from all three twentieth-century efforts. At a moment when the Christian communities need all the help they can get, it seems advisable to be in an accumulating, not a repudiating, mood.

Equally important: can "the theology of hope" as opposed to a "theology with hope" bear the weight of all that needs to be done in the decades ahead? In the hands of its most gifted interpreters such a school or mode of thought provides an opportunity for revisiting all the great themes of Christian reference. But just as easily most of these reference points can be forgotten and lost in slogans. A systematic theology of hope could result in a closure, an obsessive interest, a crusade—in short, something which would and should breed reaction. A generation which concentrates entirely on one way of doing theology will almost inevitably foreclose some possibilities, overlook some potential contributions, and be something less than catholic.

As an added accent in Christian thought, a theology with hope has something to say; it emphasizes a neglected theme. One could say that it makes little difference which of the Christian virtues is accented: let it be theology of hope, of faith, of love; let it be directed to any tense—of hope or memory or present action—it makes little difference so long as overall it is appropriate to the action of the Christian community in the future.

Those who have picked up this book in the hope that from it they can gain a capsuled all-purpose theology will have been put off by the previous paragraph. If so, it will have fulfilled its purpose: my whole argument is a criticism of nervous theology, Christian thought which is fickle, jumpy, viscous. The record of the recent past gives every reason to lose confidence in those who are too sure of cultural moods and too ready with a relevant Christian comment or style. For them, theology is like the tip of a magnetic needle: it is always able to locate the new driving forces, centers of power, or pulls of history and to point to them. Then comes the claim of relevance. For them, theology is like antennae, always ready to pick up what is in the air.

The alternative is not static conservatism. The static advocate of sameness will be frustrated by the fact that nothing remains the same: he may repeat the words of a previous generation, but these words will have acquired a new history and a new legacy, and they will mean something different and something new. Given the choice between the cult of relevance and the cult of aloof integralism, we would choose the former, for it at least bears some possibility of addressing the thought world in which today's people have to move and the world of effects which has to be the arena for their attempt to work out purpose.

The proper alternative to nervous and faddist theology would be one which is not only magnetic needle-tip but also axis; it would not only seek the ear of society but would have something to say. The word attracts misunderstandings, but it remains appropriate: theology should have something of an "aristocratic" character. It should work to some extent out of its own norms, as they are gained from revelation or speculation or tradition.

By aristocratic nothing pretentious or snobbish is meant; rather something like Lordship when applied to Christ is in place. It serves in the humblest of ways without ever losing identity or integrity. When someone taps another on the shoulder and says, in effect, "Notice me, I am relevant to you. I have listened to what you are talking about, and now that you have said it, I want to comment," he is destined to lose a hearing. Christian theology at its best issues in probes, stabs, sayings, actions, to which other forces in history have to address themselves, to become relevant.

Faddist theology forgets this. It may be in place, then, to call for theology without adjectives or prepositional phrases. On the other hand, the demands of an epoch call forth special accents in theology. Aware of this, we can examine in proper perspective the promise associated with a theology that connects itself with motifs of future and hope. Such a theology has presented itself with a power that causes many alternative options to disappear. It comes with what seems to be a logical propriety, to preempt many of the intellectual passions of Christians in this age.

Several legitimate demands of any theological accent impress themselves at once. It should be oriented toward action, as its parent has been. Unless theology is to return to the cloister and the cobwebbed corners of seminaries and if it is to make a difference in the public world, it will have to be able to be related in coalitions or by translation to people who do not share the Christian faith.

Second, an emphasis in theology would have to be able to be directed to a world of sudden change. At this moment in history it is difficult to picture the development of a truly universal theology: theology would be expressive of the life and vision of particular communities. In this case, Western Christianity is under scrutiny. But its predominant styles of thinking have to be related to that community's action toward the whole world. So it should have a bearing on the public and political lives of people in the parts of the world where Christianity remains a presence.

While the list of criteria could be extended indefinitely, still another remains prime: the coming theology should be somehow popular, people-directed, applicable to and available to wide sectors of the Christian gathering. This does not mean that it can never be treated in technical terms or that religious thinkers always have to chatter in slang and cater for popularity. Such a burden would be intolerable for those who have a mandate to probe and push. Rather, the call for a popular theology recalls the fact that we live in a social world. People's apprehension of reality, their concepts and languages and intentions, are shaped interpersonally. The needed theological accents will do justice to this social aspect of Christian apprehension. They will not be designed for Tarzans or Robinson Crusoes but for people in community, potential agents of power and change.[51]

A theology marked by the accent of Christian hope will not share the shortcomings of the Comtean-style philosophies of history that were offered as neutral secular views. Christian hope is not the same thing as "knowledge about the future." It makes no claims about the detail of tomorrow and offers no gnostic secret wisdom about the knowledge appropriate to the next moment. The historian is drawn to it precisely because it is open to every contingency; it does allow him to "wait and see" even as it calls him to action. Such Christian thought is not dependent upon an all-embracing life style, an all-pervading principle of reason ("primitive man," "religious man," "secular or technological man"). It tolerates pluralism and diversity within an epoch, reckons with disparate cultural backgrounds, and allows freedom for independent development to coexistent people and societies. In all these respects, it is more appropriate to an analytic, secular, and empirical age than were the secular theologies with their overconfidence about inclusive epochal developments.

Yet the called-for Christian thought, marked by hope, is not designed just so that people can interpret the passing parade. The potential for action and change is implicit in the term "hope" itself. Recalling the discussion of Arthur Danto and George Allan: this mode allows for "imaginative projections." In Daniel Bell's framework, here is room for writing some "as ifs," or acting on the basis of alternative scenarios. It has functions in the public, political, and personal realms.

These functions can best be illustrated by reference to an imaginative projection which does not come from the realm of formal theology. From Thomas Jefferson through Abraham Lincoln, during the crucial years of the shaping of the republic, the leaders spoke of America as "the last, best hope of earth" or of mankind. How did they know? The historian of secular bent would have to remain the analyst and say: prove it. By his definition, these great presidents could prove nothing. The future had not yet occurred. Men have to wait and see. Until the end of the human story, there is always the possibility that a later, better hope of earth might rise. That nothing greater or better could follow on America's downfall was certainly an article of faith to Jefferson and Lincoln, but the truth of the proposition was not demonstrable.

In one sense, these chief executives could be called substantive philosophers of history. They claimed to discern the meaning of history as if the outcome had already occurred. In effect: when the end of history arrives, it will be seen that America was "the last, best hope of earth." But Jefferson and Lincoln were not acting as formal philosophers but as leaders of people. They might have been embarrassed to have to debate what to them was self-evident; or they would have been too wise to become engaged in debate over what they would have known was an article of faith.

They were uttering a theology accented by hope. They were issuing a call for action. In effect, they said that the young republic was so important to the human future that the present generation had to be careful custodians of its destiny. They had to think wisely and give ultimate sacrifices. This they would not do if they did not believe in its validity.

The dangers of such an approach or a call are obvious: it can lead to messianism, manifest destiny, arrogance, exclusivism, fanaticism, self-righteousness, crusading spirit—and much more.

Despite such risks, the assets of such an imaginative projection are also obvious. It allows for the asset of worthwhileness, the claim that the destiny deserves rich investment.

Translated to the Christian scene, faith translated to assertions about hope can play the role not of philosophy of history but of alternative scenarios for future action. Jesus Christ *is* the hope of the world. This is the victory that *has* overcome the world, even your faith. The gates of death *will* not prevail. Note the present, perfect, and future tenses, all having the same function. Someone has spoken of the empirical life of the Christian community as marked by "hope projected backward." The Christian gathering moves in the light of images bounced off a screen at the end of history. It cannot demonstrate that the Church is one or holy or catholic or apostolic. It is each of these by mandate and promise, in genesis and in fulfillment, hidden under symbols of intention and frustrated by finitude in the present situation. That Christ is the hope of the world or that faith in him belongs to those who have overcome it are anything but demonstrable propositions or self-evident truths. Whatever else they are, they serve as functional equivalents to the language of the "last, best hope" theme.

That men of faith late in the twentieth century should use the language of hope is not surprising or without precedent. As noted earlier, they are only accenting a permanent, recurring, but often neglected note. The resources for that language are manifold. They take root in the Biblical language of promise and pledge. Abraham is to go out, not knowing where he is to go but with confidence, for he has his eye on the eternal city, whose builder and maker is God. He is bound to a future, not because he has a road map but because he has a promise.

The central figure in the language of promise, for the Christian, is Jesus Christ. As the foremost Protestant advocate of a hope-centered theology, Jürgen Moltmann, has put it,[52] this is hope in God "who gives life to the dead and calls into existence the things that do not exist" (Rom. 4:17, RSV); it "knows the power of negation and of the judgment over all being and its possibilities, and still it hopes. As 'crucified hope' it can become hope of the resurrection." As crucified hope, it is not an evasion of the tragic element of life: "It now performs whatever makes straight the way of the Lord; however, at the very same time, it must live through the dark night in which no one's actions are effective."

The promise was uttered in the past and Jesus Christ is a figure in history; this theology, therefore, does not have to issue in rejection of a useless past. But it does not locate revelation as a finished product belonging to dead pages of history. In a way, revelation is a category of the end and of the future. Yahweh is the future of which the prophets speak. Jesus Christ will be revealed in the future. The Christian does not claim special knowledge about what is to come, but he looks toward the future in a special way.

A theology which emphasizes future and hope reopens the question of talk about God which the secular theology had killed off ("death of God") or evaded ("moratorium on God talk"). In the reading of Ernst Bloch, the God of the Bible has "futurity as his essential feature."[53] Such a view finds God as an agent or lever in history and not as an object in a serial of objects outside history. By itself, the hope-motivated theology may not be able to come forth with a fulfilled new "doctrine of God," as some of its overenthusiastic advocates imply that it can. But it may make a contribution to the witness out of which such a doctrine or theological motif may be born for a new epoch.

In the meantime, the language of future and hope is directed to mission, service, church, revolution: it is concerned with people. Men are called to act *coram Deo,* in the sight of God, before they have worked out all details of a philosophy *versus Deum,* which moves speculatively toward God. Thus man is free for life under promise, which is mission (*pro-missio*). As before: we do not know what man is; is he godless or godly, secular or religious? He is an indeterminate being, whose essential nature remains elusive, whose fulfillment is hidden until history's outcome is known. He *is* his praxis, his mission, his hope.

A theology which is catholic but not cultic will be free from the necessity of having to become exclusive. It would be intolerable to think of all the theological work of a generation going into the attempt to build a single edifice called Theology of Hope. One protection against such an endeavor is in the pluriformity of influences behind the accents of the new generation in theology. It retains the world affirmation of liberalism and secular theology and the critical "not yet" note of the crisis theology which had intervened. It retains Friedrich Gogarten's appreciation of the Biblical momentum behind secularity and Karl Barth's criticism of self-directed religion. Notes of the Biblical "history of salvation" are revisited, though it does not seek to run *Heilsgeschichte* like a self-protected lead-encased tube through "real" history. "The Christian meaning of history is therefore the hope that secular history is also a part of that meaning which sacred history sets forth, that in the end there is only *one* history, that all history is ultimately sacred"[54] (Paul Ricoeur).

Theology which emphasizes the future and hope can tolerate ambiguity and contradiction in history. It picks up the positive note of developmental visions like Teilhard de Chardin's, but retains a humanistic note that is often lacking in a long-pull view which can reduce World War II to a footnote and see positive value in the atomic bomb. From Teilhard it learns to speak of *Dieu-en-avant,* God ahead of us. It shares Ernst Bloch's sense of "infatuation with the possible," his concern for the pull of the "not-yet," his love for the *novum* or new in history, his desire to see matter transformed by human purpose. It draws on the researches of those who study the phenomenology of hope, who try to discern man as a desiring, wishing, willing, hoping, and acting being. Not that all Christians have to study these quasi-metaphysical figures that have inspired new thought about hope: their ideas and cadences are anticipated in the Psalms, in prophets like Isaiah and Jeremiah, in the language of the future in Paul and other New Testament writers; they have been heard again and again in Christian history, usually by "fringe" (nonestablishment) people like Joachim of Flora, Thomas Müntzer, and sectarians of the Puritan period or at the time of the rise of industrialism. In Martin Luther's terms, Christians are to take their cue from the future.

Insofar as the language of Christian hope enters the Christian community's language about the future it can liberate from the tyranny of false alternatives. Optimism and pessimism, Utopia and Armageddon no longer need to dominate. They all rule out realities which a community in mission must consider.

The non-Christian does not share Christian hope and thus he may find discussion of a theological recovery which accents the future to be arcane, exotic, frivolous, or beside the point. His finding will be justified if The Theology of Hope becomes a cult or a fad, if too much energy or too much "hope" is placed in it at the expense of other resources. But if it amplifies and accents what is already present in the Christian gathering and becomes the property of the many, it can energize Christian action and the "man of good will" outside the Christian orbit will recognize its effects in the human city and the political realm.

As a movement, an all-purpose motif, or a philosophy of history the hope language has limits. It is not so original as its proponents claim it to be. It advertises a part of Christian language as if it were the whole. So far, there have been diminishing returns, especially when the hope theology seems to offer some sort of knowledge about the future. This theology, by locating transcendence always in the future (and thus, again, where it cannot be verified or checked out), will look like another cheating game of theologians unless they surround it with other forms of witness. And for many, it may have its own nihilistic tinge; as one friend put it: "Nothing ever happens. I am tired of waiting." When *The* Theology of Hope sounds like the language of Godot it fails to pick up a note of the Christian theme of promise. For Christian promise is checked out and ratified in experience. Something *does* happen. A person asks that nothing should separate him from the love of God in Christ —and nothing does. The community is sustained by witness to the fulfillment of promise. If nothing ever happened, if theology were pure future and only hope, no one would hope.

When the language of future and hope makes use of the past without becoming imprisoned by it, some experience of liberation ensues. When it calls for responsible participation in the present without demanding a compulsive sense about outcomes, it contributes to Christian freedom. When it avoids the dangers of messianism but still can convince people that their actions make a difference in the world—then the developing theology can contribute to the power situation of the world. Thereupon it has to be taken seriously by Christian and non-Christian alike.

6

The Power of Those Who Hope

*W*henever someone sets out to make a contribution to church or world there is danger that he lose perspective on himself and his project. On the other hand, there is danger that those who come into contact with his project may have difficulty locating it: how seriously should it be taken? Having argued for an ambivalent view of man, society, and history and then contended that the language of Christian hope can serve as an agent for determining their futures, it is necessary to help locate the project.

Two cartoons that I have cherished for years in my mind if not in my scrapbook may be of help. On the one hand, the world has not here been portrayed as absolutely closed off to agents of change for the good. One cartoon relates to the absurdity of hoping when it takes the form of planning in the midst of hopelessness. Shel Silverstein portrays two gaunt, bearded convicts in a very high, very narrow cell. Far above them, near the ceiling, is a window too small for even their emaciated figures to pass. As

I recall them, they are chained to the wall by arms, neck, abdomen, and legs—with no doubt a ball and chain thrown in for good measure. In the midst of this, one turns to the other and says, "Now, here's my plan!"

The political uses of future and hope, which are the subjects of this argument, do not relate to that kind of situation. Christianity has a word of personal hope to people with terminal illness or in utter despair; it believes that there is a plan for such circumstances. That does not enter in (though it does not necessarily appear in contradiction to) the concerns of this book. When the hydrogen bomb is falling on the city of man, there is only folly in the shout of the ghostly and gaunt, "Now, here's my plan!" Here we are concerned with the potential for action in dire and tragic circumstances, in a world of war and hate, hunger, pollution, and overpopulation. Can the Christian community make some contribution?

The other recalled cartoon keeps the potency of the contribution in perspective. In one version the setting is the Grand Canyon; in another, the base of Niagara Falls is the scene. A large, dominating woman and her meek, bespectacled, diminutive, and obviously henpecked husband are taking in the view. She has turned to him to say, "Makes *you* feel very insignificant, doesn't it?" When in a pluralistic and political world a person speaks out of the context of any particular religious community, he does well to have the big lady near by to remind him of how insignificant he is and feels and ought to feel.

From the viewpoint of the United Nations, the Pentagon, the tables of peace negotiations, the halls of industry, Christian witness may be beside the point—an extraneous and superfluous word. At most it may serve to complicate some issues, for it belongs to a vestigial power bloc or interest group. More likely, it is an irrelevant but respectable nostalgic reference to the days when Christians ran the show, had empire, and held power.

When talk of Christian contribution to rapid social change or even revolution is brought up, there is room for many a snort or quick dismissal. "Funny, you don't look revolutionary," people could say of the Christian community at large just as in the nineteenth century Friedrich Nietzsche could say, in effect, "Funny, you don't look redeemed!" In most places the majority of Christians act just like their neighbors. They look out for themselves, take care to become established, and defend the status quo.

Not many politicians have to worry about pressure from rural southern Protestant rednecks to legislate changes which might benefit minority races—even though these people may have sat in range of a Christian pulpit and heard Biblical texts supporting human dignity and brotherhood more faithfully than any other element in society. A northern urban Roman Catholic legislator knows very well that he will draw more support from ethnic communities where Catholic faithfulness is strong if he will only subtly veil his racism and work consistently against social legislation of the type for which their Popes have regularly been contending for seventy and more years.

In any Catholic or Protestant suburb, any superpatriot or militarist can count on the support of the vast majority of churchgoers to go along with him in absolutely any kind of military engagement fought with absolutely any kind of means toward absolutely any kind of ends: "the powers that be are ordained of God." Only a small minority will ordinarily violate the consensus. In Latin American nations, one would hardly expect ruling Catholic elites to disperse their holdings or their power for the sake of starving populations which are now subjected to every kind of indignity. One would rarely expect Christian churches in the Third World to have the luxury of distance which might permit them to transcend the militant nationalism in their own environment.

Poll-takers find negligible differences between Christians and non-Christians on any significant humane or ethical issue—and many studies reveal Christians to be further from the ethical norms proclaimed by their tradition than are "outsiders." The same poll-takers find that the majority of Christian people, at least in American society, resent the attempt by leadership to get out of the safe little cultural slot (private-personal-familial-leisure life) in which they were placed. There is disdain for the churches when they reinvolve themselves in the political order. There is distaste for any suggestion that The People of God should, as a people, take on problems in their environment.

Let the catalogue of grizzlies continue. Any observer can see that by far the vast majority of Christian energies in the world are devoted to self-service and not sacrifice for others. An analysis of parochial life (one glance at the weekly calendar in any Sunday church bulletin will suffice) will reveal that most of the time people are being trained to serve themselves. A friend who once served a group of alienated and disaffected Christians (who would have nothing to do with congregational life) learned from one of them how a congregation operates. "Suppose all of us who are employees at a large department store all arrived at nine in the morning, locked the doors, and spent that day—as every day —performing services only for each other and selling things to each other; that is what a congregation is like."

The portion of church budgets used for humane purposes is negligible in comparison to that devoted to keeping the show going. The energies devoted to adult education, while perhaps growing, still concentrate more on individualist concerns than on the action of the people of God in providing meaning, dignity, and goods for the majority of the people of the world who do not share the physical conditions of affluent, developed life. "How many divisions has the Pope?" scoffed a modern totalitarian, who wanted to set Christian power in its place. "How many enthusiasts do the Christians have?" is a legitimate put-down question directed against incipient triumphalism in Christian plans and programs for service.

In the midst of this: "Now, here's my plan!" "Makes *me* feel pretty insignificant, doesn't it?"

If hope in hopelessness in the political realm seems absurd, however, then hopelessness in the midst of hope is equally absurd. Not everything in the world is nailed down, closed up, finished off, properly put together. And the potential of Christian involvement in care of the earth, care of the person, and care of the community remains. Very often the potential is overlooked precisely because the Christian community is less interested in the search for a usable future than it is for keeping up appearances in relation to a useless past.

When the Christian community is inert, this is either because it has not yet heard, experienced, and appropriated a word of judgment and grace; or because of lethargy and inertia; or because of hardness of heart. Many men of faith have not yet been stimulated to begin to live already in the future, to see what others will later see, to be tapped for a body which has movement and momentum. If there is to be change, we must look at the actual location of power and its potential in today's Christian community. This can be done in reference to elitist power, then to the whole of the Church, and finally, power in coalition.

Elitist, first. Our survey of Christian inertia or defense of the status quo deliberately avoided reference to elites; at this point, an explicit reference to elites seems deliberately to do injustice to Christian life. What place do elites have? Are not all Christians of the same rank and status? Theologically, yes; functionally, no. There is here no hint of a desire for a recognizable elite cast or a new aristocracy. Left to themselves, elites can be more self-serving and inverted than masses are. I have brought up this term from sociology (as opposed to ecclesiology) to be sure not to understress the power of creative minorities while at the same time pointing to some of their limits.

A creative minority has a contribution far beyond its statistical weight. Ten draft-resistant sons and their supportive fathers can create a great change in the suburban church of which we spoke earlier. A few courageous proponents of urban change in an ethnic ward can keep the whole ward off balance and permit the intrusion of new hope. A theological alert leadership in a southern Protestant group can serve to counterbalance a redneck majority. This is not to say that they will always prevail; they will change history.

Thus the artist belongs to a creative minority; the Christian artist with words, like Alan Paton in South Africa or Father Alfred Delp in Hitler's Germany, can provide conscience and moral insight when thousands around him turn their backs. The thinker can be great "to the extent that he sees already what others do not see as yet."[55] Often in Christian history the thinking pioneer eventually picks up a following. The impact of the secular theology on the modes of Christian action has already been felt far beyond the expectable "front-lines" (inner-city, campus, youth movements) and has penetrated the lives of persons and cells in the worlds of business, communications, human relations, and family life. Those who are at home with the media know how the articulate and gifted few can influence the many.

So the Christian church knows the power of the influence makers: they can portray threat, suggest promise, interpret, induce, persuade, and lead to choice. They are those who are able to locate the power resources of history, to intuit meaning, to relate to human need, to work with the dynamisms by which history moves.

The role of the symbolic leader is changing in Christian circles because the role of symbols and the symbols themselves are undergoing transformation. The power of Christian leadership lies in the leaders' ability to move people in response to evocative symbols. Thus, once upon a time, the clergy could say: "Follow; if you do, you will be saved. If not, you will be damned." In theocratic and imperial ages, Christians used and misused the power to excommunicate or to interdict in order to move people. The modern Church does not have and claims not to want such powers any longer. But it does elicit response to symbols expressive of utter judgment and grace.

When Martin Luther King would stimulate change by leading a nonviolent march to call for action to change a social evil, he greatly inconvenienced many a southern sheriff. Purportedly, this was because of his magic, his talent, his widely-advertised charisma. More was involved, as King knew. No sheriff would be moved by a black man's charism—he would not be likely to regard him in any personal way. He had to deal with the fact that King's power lay in the way he appealed to the conscience of Americans, especially American Christians. They knew in their hearts and minds that the charter documents of Church and nation forbade the limits placed upon American blacks. So long as the evocative symbols which had formed that conscience had vestigial or nascent power in the lives of a hundred million Americans there was the possibility of change. The sung scenario or alternative future called "We shall overcome!" was entirely plausible.

Elites which fail to recognize the potency of those symbols live for the short run. When the Christian Church is described as a mere political action group, the limits of one kind of power are immediately obvious. The churches lack the power to tax, to draft, to coerce. They have to move people to altruistic activity, to transcendence of self, to sacrifice for others in ways congruent with Christian norms and vision.

The elites, then, relate to the world indirectly through the potency of "the whole People of God."

Reference to the whole brings to mind the limits of Christian power: there is disagreement, nominal membership, half-commitment, illiteracy, lethargy. Each of these complicates Christian participation. Because of them, it is urgent to talk about the potential before one settles for all the necessary compromises with reality. For the sake of Christian participation, they would have to be as free as possible from self-preoccupation and as free as possible to work together. This prospect would not mean the end of differences between Christians or the cutting off of creative conflict. On the contrary: without creative conflict it is likely that any body would stagnate and die. Rather, the end of irrelevant difference and meaningless conflict is called for. Secondly, Christians have to be as free as possible for creative coalition with others who share aspects of their vision. These two demands call for examination of the potential of what are usually denominated "ecumenism" and "secular ecumenism."

Today's Christian activist approaches the ecumenical topic with diffidence and disinterest. To most people it immediately evokes images of the Ecumenical Movement, in which not too much hope is placed. Such an attitude deserves examination, for the Ecumenical Movement has attracted the major Christian energies of the times and it has probably been the event which will give the name for Christians to the first two-thirds of the twentieth century. Yet it is already treated with condescension and little sense of prospect by the coming generation in the Western Church.

Make no mistake: the ecumenical achievement is already profound. In four and a half years Protestants and Catholics overcame most of the differences which had developed for four and a half centuries. In a decade Eastern and Western Christians came closer together than they had for a millennium. In context, these are magnificent moves; in isolation, they have little to offer.

The cynics see ecumenism as a Christian response to secular pressures. When people *really* believed, as our forefathers did, they were ready to cut each other's throats. Today they get along because they are all indifferent half-believers.

Others see the ecumenical result growing out of external factors like a new sociological awareness, a tactical interest, or the shaping influence of mass communications. Many see it as a centripetal, defeatist trend, "sheep huddled together because of the storm," or "price-fixing for the same market." There may be elements of all these less than glorious bases in ecumenism. It would be hard to picture the reform of any movement without some external pressures first. But there is much countertestimony to the idea that these aspects exhaust the ecumenical reality.

To move past the ecumenical stasis it would be a good idea if those who seek a usable future would regard the Ecumenical Movement as already completed and fulfilled for all practical purposes. Such action is not for the purpose of creating illusion or frustrating those who are involved in mopping-up operations so much as it is designed to make use of a unity that patently does exist.

Christians whose consciences have been aroused would not be likely to be content with remaining elements which contribute to separation, nor would they be content with halfhearted compromise over differences. But the majority of them have to see that the remaining differences are best left to committees assigned the task of technical negotiating. It may be a sinful luxury for the rest of Christian people to sit idly by while these specialists work out arrangements. Norman Cousins, during frustration over Viet-

namese war negotiations in Paris, once argued that these con-
ferences should be relocated on battlefields in Vietnam. So with
ecumenical committees: they should meet in dialogue with students on secular campuses, or in buses on the way to poverty programs or in burned-out motels in ghetto riot areas. Until they do,
those who are at home with coffee-houses, poverty marches, and
ghetto riots cannot wait.

To see ecumenical committees as mopping-up artists does
sound condescending; it is designed to sound merely reportorial.
It is a simple fact that the Ecumenical Movement is not a young
people's movement any more: it neither asks nor answers the
questions of a coming generation. Born of lay, student, and missionary impulses, the movement had to become technical and
clerical in its later stages. Most Christian people are interested
onlookers at best.

The generations may only be engaging in leapfrogging at this
point. What the son wants to forget the grandson wants to re-
member: if today's young Catholic accepts the gifts of the generation of the Congars, the de Lubacs, the Karl Adams, without
retracing the difficult steps which made the gift possible, no doubt
his children—if the Church survives in any recognizable form—
would be more ready to take a look back at the era that led up
through Vatican II. For now, the generation of Christians begins
from a pan-Christian point of view.

From the viewpoint of the younger lay and clerical leaders, the
Ecumenical Movement became rationally programmatic, "linear," involved with negotiated compromise on apparently irrelevant issues. As such, it belonged to the exhausted tradition and
contributed to the sense of a useless past. If the basic issue is the
problem of God and the basic trauma deals with belief and un-
belief, it is hard for a generation to be concerned with the questions as to who holds to the *filioque* clause today, or whether
Lutherans and Zwinglians can fit their way back into the mentality of the Marburg conference of 1529.

Stated more positively, the coming generation has accepted the
gift and pays the highest testimony of taking the achievement and
putting it to work. When a great jet has too much power to stay

on the runway and must take off, no matter what is in the way, a flight officer shouts, "V-One!" From then on, the pilot cannot abort. The Ecumenical Movement found the churches in a V-One stage: destination uncertain, obstacles ahead threatening, crew not necessarily stable, passengers contentious. But from the viewpoint of the outsider, they all now shared a common destiny.

The Ecumenical Movement did make possible a new arrangement of power. This is meant not in the old sense that its critics implied: that it tried to gather more millions of people, so that it could have better public relations, better reputation, more weight to throw around. Rather, the new arrangement of power suggests that more kinds of Christian people can draw on more kinds of resources to fill more kinds of needs. When this occurs, Christians live within the mandates (be one!) and the promise (you shall be one!) which are the origin and the fulfillment of the Church. Between, all is becoming, all is process, nothing is finished or perfect or complete.

The use of ecumenical achievement allows the world to become a magnet once again. The world presents so many problems and possibilities that no portion of the Church has the resources to meet them all or the scope to appropriate them all. Thus the Western churches have learned much about the conditions of Christian existence in Soviet and Central European lands by contact with Eastern Orthodox Christians, who would have been hidden from view apart from ecumenical endeavor. In the Western Church, Protestant Christians have taken on responsibility for Latin America in ways they could not have when there was hostility with Catholics, and Catholics have come to terms with the North American ethos where they had been in the minority for much of four and a half centuries. Interactive Protestant groups have enriched, not impoverished, their vocabularies and potential services because of their ecumenical entente.

Substantive issues remain to separate Christians. Not all matters relating to the disputes over grace and authority in the sixteenth century have been settled between Protestants and Catholics. They will not be settled, however, by going backward and living in the past. "Why don't Catholics repeal the Council of Trent on grace?'' ask the pickier Protestants who want to write the rules. "Why should they?'' ask those who read the footnotes on grace in *The Jerusalem Bible* or who listen to evangelical Catholic sermons. The grace question is obscured by, but will probably be faced only along with, the God-question in the late twentieth century. On authority: it has now been seen that Protestant polity has not always been a protection against authoritarianism and unfreedom, and it is now clear that Catholic authority is learning to move by persuasion, not coercion, in the modern world. There are patent areas of convergence among people who are trying to transcend past ways of putting the problems and to accept the gifts of their own age as resources toward solution.

Frustrations remain. Residual differences keep some Christians from others' central eucharistic rites and sacraments. But the pace of change here, too, is swift and sudden. A new generation has also learned how to take direction on these fronts and not to wait for committees to settle everything before they set out to express their evident one-ness. They have little sense for meaningless, accidental ecclesiological inheritances: why should a young Catholic ghetto worker commune with a backlashing Catholic, with whose world view and theology he will never agree, he asks— and then be frustrated in his desire to share the sacrament with an Episcopalian or Lutheran whose view of life and whose theology he does share?

What has been spoken for here is not a new indifferentism but a higher differentism; not a casual disregard for church discipline but a revision of it. Why excommunicate Catholics for violating a minor law of the Church but not for violating the Gospel itself, by being racist? Why congratulate the Protestant who keeps the laws of his church but remains a slum landlord? These are the questions asked by a generation with a post-ecumenical consciousness.

The energies once devoted to ecumenism are now being directed by those who want to shape a future, to what some have called—in a rather unfortunate coinage—secular ecumenism. In Father Avery Dulles' terms,[56] this meant for the Church to be "more in touch with contemporary secular man . . . less tuned in upon itself, more open to the world and its concerns." For those concerns to be operative, Christians have found it important to form *ad hoc* alliances and coalitions with people who do not share their faith. These alliances are not formed for the purpose of Christian apology or for covert evangelism, though the exposure may very well mean a better understanding of Christian purpose, and thus a step toward evangelization. They exist chiefly, however, to accomplish specific goals.

If Christians wish to enact their vision of free and open societies in the future; if they wish to see that the physical needs of more people are met, and that institutions which guarantee them dignity and purpose evolve, they seek the others who share something of these goals. When such alliances are fashioned, Christians reveal that they do not claim a monopoly on social justice or virtue; in fact, they are thereby admitting that they are incapable of taking on these tasks alone.

In advocating such alliances we come to the most easily misunderstandable portion of this book. There is here no interest in devising a "Christian party in politics" or a new coalition with a Christian center. The advocacy does not imply that the work of *ad hoc* coalitions exhausts all the purposes of the Church. Many Christian activities will be undertaken only by Christians—no one else will be interested or have the motivation to do them. The Church serves to integrate people into some framework of meaning or interpretation. It provides a supportive fellowship. Recognizing that open confrontation to change on all fronts at all times is intolerable, it works to help people organize their responses. For these tasks, alliance with non-Christians is not always necessary or desirable. The coalition is chiefly for the public life of the Church.

Here there is no question of the Church completely losing its identity. Calls for such a loss have a curiously romantic bias for the existence of entities in a realistic political world. While the Church may have been overpreoccupied with self-preservation at the expense of mission, the talk about achieving all the purposes of the Church in the world by the complete giving up of identity, continuity, and form would mean guaranteeing that "what is everybody's job is nobody's job."

One more hazard: it is possible that in these coalitions the Church can be exploited or it can exploit others. It may be misused and may desire to misuse others. These are risks inherent in all alliances, in all of life. They can be avoided by careful people.

What is advocated is the idea of doing what the situation demands. Christians would work with those who have least to lose in the passing of the old orders and the old ways and who would have the highest moral, personal, and social motivations for developing the new. The goal would be to help make dissenting minorities into potentially effective majorities.

At the same time, Christians would have to bring protesting and prophetic concern to the secular coalitions, for were they to become part of effective majorities they would constitute a new establishment. The vitality, uncertainty, and general cantankerousness of the members of the various groups in the cluster should guarantee that lethargy would not set in prematurely!

Among the clusters would be the blacks, the first group we noticed in the family of dissent earlier. Many of them are Christian, acting on fundamentally Christian motivations; they are already part of the dissenting Christian minority. In the years ahead the ability of black Christians and non-Christians will be tested. For the sake of black identity it seems to be necessary that there be a passage through a stage of self-segregation. Some white Christians have accepted this practical course and adopted an ideology to go with it, as if permanent tension and segregation were Christian goals. But separation is temporary and penultimate on the way to reconciliation. At the same time, external circumstances could change the black mood instantly. For instance, were an overtly repressive or fascist regime to gain power in America, isolationist blacks and dissenting white Christians could unite the morning after. Meanwhile, Christians who are nonblack can work on alliances where possible, on interpretation where fruitful, on waiting where necessary.

The dissenting academy with its new kinds of students and professors has turned out to be an ally of prophetic Christianity in many recent causes. The opposition to the fact and the mode of American involvement to the war in Vietnam was almost entirely in the hands of students allied with faculty and clergy. While the moral vision of many of the young dissenters is studiously secular and while many of them fear alliance with the Church because of the possibility of seeing discontent bought off through a covert establishment, they have begun to regard the identifying clergy as men who have come to serve them. A real respect has grown up between college chaplains and the war resistance movement, between many clergy or religious and young people who carry their protest against society into positive action, for example in service in programs for the ghetto.

The modern university, when in alliance with the military or the industrial order, is as much of an establishment as the Church ever was; perhaps it is more interlocked with establishmentarian purposes than is the less secure Church. For this reason those in the academy who want to break off the alliance with what they see to be a dehumanizing force have found that the Church offers sanctuary, counsel, inspiration, and aid.

The poor should easily be able to relate to those in the Church who wish to bring about change. Yet it is difficult to bring about the linkage. The poor in a society like that of America have been so hidden from view, so sequestered in Appalachia or in black and white ghettos, that few channels of communication exist between them and those who would represent the re-formed Church. A relation of trust can be developed only over a long period of years. Communication of ideas is necessarily slower than it is with the affluent discontented on campuses, or with the literate heads of movements for black identity. For some years, church leaders may be representing the poor without receiving much response or reciprocation. There will be little complaint; the Christians who identify with the poor from which their Church once sprang know that the poor deserve to be faced on their own terms and never for their political potential. At the same time, Christians who have worked to develop slum tenant unions and organizing centers for the poor have been impressed at the potential for change inherent in those who are now left out in an affluent society.

The new media people, the New Left, the lonely mavericks, the secular service agencies—all of these represent the kind of dissent with which one kind of Christian has been linking up. They do not as of now have the power to outvote conservative forces like the established labor union (though newly organized groups like teachers, nurses, and others in labor forces may be breaking up the established scene) and the old political parties, but they have begun to express themselves as a second or alternative force to face those who represent the old consensus. Together they have gained courage from some small successes to work together for a radically different kind of future than envisioned by those who represent the status quo.

The small successes that have inspired further probing have not always occurred only because forward-looking Christians have dealt with restless blocs of people in society. Just as often they have come about because individual persons have responded surprisingly to new circumstances, because the previously apathetic have learned to see opportunity for change and have accepted it. Only the impatient would overlook the potential in strategically located persons and small groups. But only the romantic would overestimate this potential and would neglect the necessity of allying with other societal forces made up of people who cannot share all aspects of Christian hoping.

7

The Pressure of the Future

*R*evolution—no other word dominates discussion of change as does this one. For some the call to revolution is made prematurely and impatiently, almost as if all alternatives issue in boredom. For others talk about revolution comes as easily as tea-party chatter: affluent intellectuals with academic tenure or clerics at a safe distance from potential trouble seem to adopt revolutionary talk as one means of asserting that they can understand the world of change, are not afraid of it, and can seize the initiative in facing it. For still others, it represents apparently the only means of bringing about a situation wherein men can have and know dignity, value, and access to the basic goods of life.

The call to revolution has been with the world for two centuries, and it has a reminiscence that reaches much deeper into history than that. But it has taken a new turn since World War II, with the refinement of weapons technology and electronic devices. Whereas in the past, established governments and classes had some advantage over revolutionary forces, today the gap is vast. The powers that be are able to engage in surveillance unimagined earlier; they can control the media and thus buy off discontent and spread propaganda. In an age of sophisticated weaponry, disaffected classes stand little chance of gaining the advantage.

Despite the raising of the stakes and the increase in the odds, discontent has not lessened. For the forces which have worked to make powers-that-happen-to-be more secure and efficient have also made possible the dream of radical change and revolution. To begin with, technology itself. Once the logic of technology begins to make its way in the world, it proceeds almost relentlessly. When it confronts a new culture, the majority of the people want to share its not unmixed benefits.

Those who argue that there will be limits to the desire of the technological reach can perform a simple test. Given, on the one hand, a people's destiny to be made up of short lives, unproductive labor, little nutritious food, no comforts, virtually no security, bad health, little leisure; on the other, let there be the promise of longer lives, meaningful or productive work, good food, considerable comfort, security, health, and leisure—what, over the long pull, will they choose?

Some victims of the affluent technological order may reply, in a spirit of cynicism, nihilism, anomie, or regret: the former. Not likely; for those who have not had the psychic problems that go with the mixed physical blessings of an industrialized technological order are not likely to conceive or imagine what they can be. They lack the Marxist critique of such an order; they have empty stomachs and would like food—that is the first concern. No romantic or Luddite talk from the developed West is likely to rob them of that first desire. Nor will they be able to have only select elements of that order: if they want health or food they will find themselves skeined into a complex of technological research and production.

New people are given the choice through mass media of communication; the radio, in developing nations, or television, in American ghettos, are often the first intrusions of technology in their orbits. And these media portray a world of things; the result has been the well-publicized but little understood "revolution of rising expectations." People began to acquire the ability to hope and the right to hope when they had come the first step past utter hopelessness. And when rising expectations reach them and symbolic leaders come on the scene to help them give expression to their new-found hopes, the first seeds of revolutionary potential are present.

Almost everywhere that Christian agents of change will want to work in the world, such symbolic leaders are already present. That is why it is true that no doubt for some time to come Christians will not be able to talk about the quest for usable futures without finding that the major symbol of entrance to a meaningful future for most people has already been established: revolution! This word exerts, as it were, a pressure from the future, limiting the number of possibilities in the present.

The pressure from the future assures that the present will be seen to be intolerable. The first impulse is to revolt, out of rage, resentment, and impatience. Revolt involves "the casting off of allegiance or obedience" to someone who has ruled and "a change of opinion or of side." During the period of waiting, there will be great discontent, for an alternative way of life has been proffered but is not yet in range. Physical goods by themselves will not satisfy: making rice-Christians out of those on the verge of revolt only stimulates more eventual discontent. When President Johnson, in his state of the union address in 1968, chronicled all the physical benefits of life in his society, he pondered, then, "Why all this restlessness?" He spoke in a year when young people were playing a recording about a girl's parents, wondering why she left home—"We gave her everything money could buy." The present, no matter what the bribe and the physical promise, remains intolerable. All the circumstances of life must change.

Many people in affluent societies have chosen to identify with people on the verge of revolt. An uncomprehending affluent establishment of parents and governors asks how this can be. Why not encourage oppressed people to express themselves through the ballot box?

Inability of people who have undergone successful revolution to empathize with those who have not is proverbial. Paul Tillich liked to point out that the *least* revolutionary group in the United States, the one least likely to have understood our own revolution, is the group known as the Daughters of the American Revolution.[57] Robert McAfee Brown has put it well: those who hold four aces are not likely to ask for a new deal. They may possibly change from security, however, if they find that the house next door to the one in which they are playing is burning. Therefore, the first task of change-agents is to alert all the members of apparently secure societies that they cannot remain secure while others are not. The American suburbanite is finding out that his own livelihood is affected in fires in the city which he abandoned for residence but where he still works. The American businessman knows that he is affected by revolution in other nations. The immediate reaction of both is to set out to suppress revolt, to postpone the fire, to call for law and order or counterrevolutionary fire-power, without meeting the circumstances which brought about discontent and revolt.

What many have not yet faced and what divides them from those who speak in favor of change is one basic fact: that the gap between the have and have-not nations of the world is growing, not narrowing; that the gap between the have and have-not people of the United States is widening; it is not being closed. Robert Heilbroner has pointed out that most people of the world have to accomplish in two decades what the West accomplished not without bloodshed in two centuries.[58] Most of these people in "the Great Ascent" are nonwhite, and not likely to identify with an America where the racial gap is broadening and empathy decreasing. They are not likely to become trustful of an America whose foreign policy commits it to the support of every kind of rightist dictator, so long as he represents status quo and opposes revolutionary nationalism. And so long as these circumstances exist, Americans will continue to withdraw in confusion into new isolationism or counteract in bewilderment and confusion, as they did in Southeast Asia.

For an understanding of the impulse to revolt, one can profit from examining three dimensions of revolution once outlined succinctly by Paul Ricoeur. They are the dimensions of human civilization itself.[59]

First is the level of *goods,* instruments, machines, techniques, knowledge, and all that contribute to the comfort, wealth, and health of the community. Concerning this, intransigent Christians like to remind their activist brothers that the Church ought to deal with the spiritual, not the material needs of man. The reply to that charge is simple: the Matthaean judgment-day parables are confined almost wholly to what man did on the level of goods toward his brother. Christians are involved in this issue.

The second level is that of *institutions*—through them the goods and techniques are put to work; "institutions" imply all political and government forces and the private means of guaranteeing access to goods and power on a sustained basis. At this place the establishment-oriented Christian who may have been won over on the first point issues a rejoinder: yes, goods are all right. We have the precedent of the Good Samaritan. But that has nothing to do with regularizing access to them, seeing to distribution, etc. Here one can invoke the prophets with their call for kingdoms in which God's people would see to righteousness, equity, justice, and peace. But, following a little application of William Lee Miller, one could also work with the Good Samaritan story. Suppose each day passers-by would be beat up by thieves and robbers on the same road. Would the parable credit the Good Samaritan if he only stood by to see the evil happen each day—and then to gain some points by pouring on wine and oil and paying the hospital bill? More profitably, he would serve others by institutionalizing a solution to the robber problem!

The third level or point of involvement has to do with *values,* the approaches and attitudes of men toward each other, toward work, community, happiness, and meaning. It is hard to picture any kind of Christian complaining about the involvement of the believing community in the matter of values.

To say that there will be revolution and revolt and that Christians will somehow be a part of the world in which they occur is some distance from beginning to depict just how they might legitimately and rightfully be participants. Christian involvement begins in self-examination and preparation. One would hope that the churches would take part not in order to attract attention, to be relevant, to assert their virility, but because of human need expressed in the situation. Nor need Christians step out of their role and stop being the Church. They do not exist in order to become a revolutionary (or antirevolutionary) political party but to do what situations demand, and situations demand more things and other things than being revolutionaries.

Christians cannot, however, fulfill their missions and mandates without coming to some sort of terms with that aspect of life covered by the term revolution or radical social change. The alternative is to put oneself *a priori* on the side of the status quo, no matter how evil and dehumanizing it be. In that instance, it would be hard to picture Christians speaking at all of the future of man. They have then opted for stagnation, slavery, and death. Some Christians take the opposite tack and claim that Christianity is always and only revolutionary and that it alone can contribute the utterly and consistently novel approach in human affairs. Some spokesmen of the theology of hope or the even more recent "theologies of revolution" choose this curiously triumphalist language.

Hannah Arendt in *On Revolution* has replied to the claim that all modern revolutions are essentially Christian, even when in the hands of atheists. The claim was made, she says, because of the rebellious nature of Christian sects, the promise of the Kingdom, and the accent on equality. Miss Arendt points out that some sort of secularization must occur before the onset of modern revolutions. The fact is that no revolution was made in the name of Christianity prior to the modern age, "so the best one can say in favor of this theory is that it needed modernity to liberate the revolutionary germs of the Christian faith, which obviously is begging the question."[60]

At the same time, she does speak of some specific Christian contributions, like the linear and purposeful view of history. And she seizes upon a paraphrased quotation from Luther which does well explain the roots and limits of Christian participation. "The most permanent fate of God's word is that for its sake the world is put into uproar. For the sermon of God comes in order to change and revive the whole earth to the extent that it reaches it."[61]

Over against this view the conservative argument runs, following undialectically the witness of Paul in Romans 13, that Christians are to support any kind of government in all kinds of circumstances. They may amplify this view by pointing to the stabilizing potential in religion: someone should represent some sort of secure or heavy weight to keep society from anarchy: let other forces be prophetic or rebellious against it.

At times Christians can relate to establishment; they do pray for good order and civil concord—and there is no reason to say that the Church can never momentarily celebrate their presence. But such relating is done, in the spirit of I Corinthians 7, "as if not." There is to be a spirit of semidetachment, a potential for disengagement. And more characteristic would be Christian criticism of past human achievements, including good order—especially in the world as we have described it, where good order means good for the few and order means slavery for the many.

The Christian involvement in change goes through several stages. The first of these can be stated quite simply: preach the word! This prophetic injunction guarantees that the agents of change will be judged as much as is the rest of the world that they are to put into uproar and set out to change. The whole prophetic tradition finds the men of God speaking to and against the king, the judges, the priests, the powers that be, in the name of and under pressure from the future or the coming day of the Lord or coming Kingdom. The New Testament finds Jesus giving voice to the discontented poor. He disengages himself from the dying political order in face of the new age. King Herod can be dismissed in two words: "That fox!"—hardly a text for an American Legion Day address. Caesar? Jesus hurries past Caesar in the face of Jews who are (and should not be) carrying around to their embarrassment an image of a god, a divinized emperor on a coin. Past Caesar comes the main point: ". . . and render to God the things that are God's."

The New Testament letters find struggling young communities in need of establishment and in at least two of them there is strong endorsement of Roman loyalty, though in Revelation 13 the Christian community is seen reverting to subversive language.

Later Christians, then, inherit a dialectical tradition. All things being equal, the state over the long pull is an order created for good: support it as God's instrument. But obey God rather than men. Today's Christians also have one difficulty the prophets did not have. Jeremiah could go to the king. He knew where power lay. Today church people "are" the king; they share the power. To preach as the prophets did means going to many levels in the political order.

The second level calls for actual inconveniencing of someone. Evil in the Biblical tradition is eventually personified. While contemporary sociology, in a characteristic barbarism, allows room for some to hold that "evil resides also in impersonal institutionalized structures," in the Christian tradition one looks for the personal locus of power. "The buck stops here," either with Herod or with all Jerusalem which stones the prophets or with disciples of little faith. Somewhere there are enemies of the good who can be faced and inconvenienced. Until these enemies are actually inconvenienced, the word has not been heard, the law of God has not begun to create effect. Someone, something, must be changed.

For the Christians who fall into range of this argument, in the Western world, there is a parallel point: we ourselves must be inconvenienced. We belong to the "four aces" culture and are almost everywhere identified with the old order, the colonial-imperial powers, the "have" classes. The great exceptions are the majority of American black Christians and what would still have to be called the peasant society of Roman Catholic reminiscence in Latin America.

Preach the word: this causes "uproar" in Luther's term; upheaval and inconvenience are first stages. But the major contribution from Christians follows: they are to innovate. Here is where the Christian parallel to talk of revolution comes; this is the authentic pressure from the future. At this point I part company with those who say that Christians must identify with revolutionaries in order to change circumstances. As humans and even as Christians they may or they may not find this the best way to do so. But their activity in that respect may not be distinctively Christian and may even be problematic from a Christian ethical point of view.

Revolution may actually be "conservative"; it is an established, two centuries' old pattern of relatively minor yield and rare success. If it has taken on an autonomous life and Christians are merely to be relevant to it or cheerleaders for it—what is their distinctive contribution? Where will there be guarantees that revolutionary parties will then be judged; what will prevent them from becoming a new status quo? These are legitimate questions, designed to keep Christians from a new pathetic spirit of eagerness to belong to "what's happening" or to be "where the action is" without prior regard for the good of people or action congruent with Christian claims.

The newer theologians impressed with the language of hope like to speak of God as "the absolute future."[62] If he is the absolute future and brings creation out of nothing, this reference point ought to be an inexhaustible source of innovation in the world. I do not mean here to lapse into futurist jargon: once again, historical precedent and present possibility provide the models, paradigms, possibilities, images, and words out of which the new alternative scenarios are to be written. Rather, the innovative principle sees to it that Christians are not tyrannized by false alternatives: defense of the old order on one hand or uncritical defense of unjudged revolutionaries on the other. They are to represent a new age, a new order, a new people, a new creation—and even revolution may very well belong to the old age, the dying world. Given the new weapons and the potential for escalation of any revolution into world-wide chaos, the stakes have been raised and it may be time for newer ideas than the two centuries' old precedents.

For these and other reasons, "to innovate" seems a more appropriate category for Christians than is "to engage in revolution." Innovators may have no recourse but to engage in radical revolution: that is one of many possibilities. On the other hand, as historian Carl N. Degler[63] has said of the milder American Revolution in two chapter headings, "revolutionaries can be conservative" and "conservatives can be innovators." In the case of the American Revolution, the radical revolutionary contribution was minimal and conventional. The conservative innovation did produce a "new" nation which at its better moments could be thought of as the last, best hope of earth.

Innovation, which follows upon upheaval, has several meanings. Many people associate it with the third definition in the Oxford English Dictionary: "to bring in or introduce novelties; to make changes *in* something established." But Christianity, with reference to a God who is absolute future, moves in line with the second definition: "to bring in (something new) for the first time, to introduce as new." And, then, the first one: "to change into something new."

Dedication to the innovative principle should be more radical than alternatives. Karl Marx in his philosophy of history lets history, in effect, come to an end "inside history"; so do all Utopias. The Christian faith cannot conceive of such a moment: the pressure from the future suggests that even revolution may not bring in a full and final resolution of history. Christians want to remain sufficiently disengaged so that they can carry change further than through a revolution.

To take such a stand does not solve the problem of what to do with existing revolutions. It is hard to conceive that Christians could make up their minds in advance about the legitimacy of particular revolts. In any case, revolution would be the ultimate word, the last resort, and not the first word—as it has come to be in the mouths of many who have grown nihilistic. Revolution in the modern world means violence and violence means killing. It means that someone else is *de trop* for me and my party. We cannot coexist in the same world. I must vanquish him and kill him; I must end his potential. Inevitably, along the way, many innocents will be killed as the result of my action. This is the language of death, of the old.

Several problems present themselves, then, to Christians who call for revolution. For one thing, they may find themselves in the middle of one. Parts of the world that had once looked secure and removed from revolutionary possibility no longer remain so. A simple test: picture the twenty or thirty people most important to you, particularly if they are defenseless and "innocent." Then picture them killed by *plastique,* grenades, napalm, or bacterial warfare. If one is easily ready to pay that price, he may not likely be trusted should a revolution become successful. Is he equipped to recognize or contribute to a humane order?

A second hazard: one might win a revolution. That is, after the conflict there might come success and with it a new establishment. The Christian has to be prepared for this dangerous stage, for here—in a protestant reading of history—is where idols and icons develop; it is against one's own establishment that the prophetic word is most to be directed. But there is a third hazard: one might lose a revolution. In some parts of the world—one pictures much of Asia or Latin America—matters could not get much worse through such a loss. But in a nation like the United States an attempt at revolution, whether by blacks or any other party, would almost certainly issue in a repressive and probably fascist counterrevolution, "final solutions" to racial problems, and Big Brother control. Many of revolutionary sentiment say that they know this to be true, that they are only fighting a temporary war of preventive genocide. It is questionable whether such nihilism could be squared with an innovative Christian spirit, for it rules out all possibilities except death for all, or at least for the previously most oppressed, while many of the oppressors would live.

When all the reckoning has been done, however, it could be that the innovative Christian may find himself with no alternatives but to take part in revolution. This was the case of many French Christians in 1789, of many Europeans in 1830, 1848, 1870–71; of many Russians in 1905 and 1917; of many Americans—who revolted with far less justification from the Christian point of view than do many restless people today!—in 1776. Those who in America speak for absolute defense of powers that be in absolute rejection of revolution rarely are willing to face the ethical complication of the American revolt. In any instance, we are arguing that at times people are confronted with few alternatives. The range of possibility has narrowed. Revolution is imminent or present. Only two choices are offered: to fight for an evil and oppressive regime or to take sides with a potentially better side.

The ethics of revolutionary involvement are particularly problematic for those who advocate a nonviolent approach. They do not believe that military action solves as much as it purports to; they do not believe that a man has a right to arrogate to himself the decision concerning who should live and who should die. He knows that violence demands the end of the potentiality of another creature—a person who may himself have been able to contribute to the world's good.

At the same time we know history's dirty secret: that in many senses history = violence and violence = history. Without implied violence the political order would be both unnecessary and ineffective. Quite properly St. Paul associates magistrate with "sword"—the political order does not proceed without threat of coercion. Normally, the implied violence is not ethically problematic, for the art of governing well is to be able to exercise restraint and not to use "the sword."

The pure pacifist, if he is really consistent, must overlook or act in spite of this secret of history. As a purist, he will in the end have to be passive in the face of history's driving forces; he must be the victim and abandon himself and others to the mercies of those who are armed and want to deprive him of life. In the next chapter we shall explore the political potential of nonviolence. For now it is necessary to note that there are few pure pacifists. When one wants to enter the political arena in any way at all, he copes with the potential of the breakdown of peace or of politics and the possibility that violence, which means killing, will ensue—and he will be a part.

In this dilemma it seems possible only to say that unless one is an absolute pacifist and thus a mere victim of history or unless he is a conscienceless advocate of violence, and thus a killer, the call for revolutionary action has to be a last resort. This means that there cannot be a decision in advance concerning the legitimacy of violence. I argue that killing never becomes "right" whether in mere war or in just war. All soldiering must be done penitently and even remorsefully; the gung-ho military spirit seems at no point to square with Christian views of intentionality and potentiality, even though it found its place among the people of God before the "new commandment" to love one another and to love the enemy was enacted.

Ricoeur, himself impressed with the political potential in nonviolence, has described the violent moment as a time when an "ethics of distress" is invoked.[64] This seems to be preferable to an ethic which anticipates the legitimacy of either killing or pure passivism and the adoption of the victim-role. No conventional ethical norms can be applied: here is "situational" ethics in which "one must do what one must do and then say one's prayers."[65]

In a revolutionary age, however, some things can be said for those who must as a last resort react in violence. The most important is to notice that ordinarily violence has been present in the prerevolutionary situation. Relations between slum landlord and his victim already imply deprivation, indignity, ill health, rats, disease—and death. The relation between right-wing elites in Latin America and the vast majority of the people in those nations where "peasant" or proletarian rights are few is already one of violence. Revolution there is conceivably a minimization or shortening of the duration of the violent period.

Compensatory violence in such circumstances may actually reduce the violence of the situation by bringing the one-sided "killing" to an early and abrupt end. If these situations seem remote, one need only recall the slave trade, death on the slave ships, and the thousands of deaths which went with being a slave in the southern United States before the Civil War to see that violence is already present in many situations where it is not apparent. When slaves revolted, as they did against tremendous odds with little hope and much courage on several occasions, a terrified master-society (in order to justify new repression) accused those who revolted of introducing killing and violence. One might well argue that had they been successful they would have prevented much killing and violence.

When all is said and done, however, the "ethics of distress" seems to be a better alternative than is a "theology of revolution" which sets out in advance to justify the principle of revolution.

The pressure from the future which has led many to see revolution as the only step exerts itself in many ways on Christians. Not all social change has to be undertaken through violent means. Intellectual guerrilla warfare is one alternative: properly located spokesmen for change can achieve much which armed revolutionaries cannot; there are usually strong governmental intelligence and police forces to put down the Che Guevaras. There is less possibility that a combination of such forces can put down the moral leaders who may suffer for their convictions, but whose argument eventually wins the day.

Nor should the power of persuasion be underestimated. While Latin American and Asian masses are not free to persuade, American blacks are on the verge of being able to do so, and white American rebels are certainly free to work through other means. The call for revolution is often the mark of the incompetent and the defeated. Having failed, they want others to go down with them. Or not having tried, they will try the last resort first. People act from a variety of motives, including altruism. When a member of the American middle class joins the New Left and assumes that economic determinism marks the lives of all, he is himself in a way a living refutation of his own view. Some moral vision must have reached him to issue in change; has he tried to examine the teleology of his own moral experience and attempted to effect change in others? Or, having seen the light and becoming impatient, must he chart another avenue for change for the rest of society?

Those who recall the line that "conservatives may be innovators" could dismiss some of my remarks as being acquiescent or counterrevolutionary. To them I can only say: reread this chapter and see if at any point there is an endorsing of the status quo anywhere. The question is not support of the old—the Christian is committed to the new creation and thus to innovation. The question has to do with effective and ethical means. In the end a Dietrich Bonhoeffer turns violent and plots the death of Hitler.

In the end Father Camilo Torres takes to the hills and dies with the guerrillas. One hopes they were both discontented with anything short of an "ethic of distress" in which there is room for self-judgment even as there is experience of grace.

8

A Scale of Responses

$\mathcal{I}$f man is an indeterminate be-
ing, open with his society to both religious and secular symbols,
and if the Christian Church sets out to judge and to redeem in
both the religious and secular dimensions, then the part of a re-
newed Christianity in the political order is assured, at least in the
immediate future. The first test of this participation was the most
extreme one: revolution. But revolution is not necessarily the
only context of politics. Even the revolutionaries are ready to contend that if they come to success a new revolution would not be
necessary. For most people or societies revolution may be a once-
in-a-century or at most a once-in-a-lifetime trauma.

Meanwhile, the political order lives on in the day-to-day world,
and for this less dramatic ethical realm Christian resources can
more readily be brought into play. If the word proclaimed by the
Church is to create uproar and inconvenience and then to follow
through with innovation, this function ought to be even more

meaningful in the political and social realm where routine is deadening and where stagnation can result.

By beginning with revolution it is possible to speak of the normal political realm as one of reasonable noncontroversiality. Anything but that is the case, and by no means all Western Christians are convinced that the churches should involve themselves with this order. If they do not, they may take little part in devising and shaping a future worthy of man. Never mind, say the critics. The task of the Church is either to rescue people out of the world and to teach them not to be tainted by the socio-political world, or it is to reshape individuals, separate them from the people of God, and send them in isolation or as lonely citizens to effect reform in the world.

These criticisms have a solid base and deserve a hearing. For the first, one recalls that there are those who see the Church only as an action agency. Whenever people try to see the Church "only" as something or other, they tend to throw away something of catholic value. Unless the "soul"—to use a word newly in vogue again—the inner being, the spiritual man is faced with the demands of the sacred and fed with the word of grace, it is not likely that much of a spiritual capital will be built up. The power of God comes to men as that which makes something of nothing, which creates forgiven and free men where there had been guilty and enslaved men, which provides possibility where there had been only despair—and a church which wavers from proclaiming this power will risk losing all kinds of powers. The political activists tend to live off a spiritual capital in which they do not reinvest. In short, it is both unfair to Christian people to let the Church be only one thing and it is politically naïve to assume that the Church will have any kind of power if people do not find in it a source of values and a center where their destiny is shaped and where they acquire meaning.

The other charge, that the Church should not "as a body" be involved with politics but it may have a mandate to send people in isolation into the world, is more complex. Quite often one can safely nurture the impression that this point of view is born because the particular spokesman disagrees with a particular stand taken by the Church. During the years when the American Protestant churches were working for legislation beneficial to themselves or capable of preserving their way of life—as in the case of prohibition, antibirth control, antigambling, and Sabbath laws —few such complaints were heard. Then it was merely assumed that the churches were supporting morality as such, accidentally taking the legal route to fulfill moral claims. More recently, when church leadership—shocked at racial policies, urban development, and American military programs—came into a position of dissent, reactionary forces spoke up.

Such reaction is understandable; it is part of the give-and-take of politics. God is invoked on each side—by some, on behalf of change in a social contract which deprives people of dignity and opportunity; by others, on behalf of retention of the old social contract, which has guaranteed privilege and advantage or at least security for those who criticize the new-style political involvements. But one naïve or deceptive feature in the reactionary critique demands evaluation.

Critics of churchly involvement often assume that if the preachers would not "preach politics"—if there would not be any meddling—*then* the political realm could remain autonomous and the churches would be uncompromised and untainted. Such a situation is not possible, however. In a political world there is no space between political positions. Not to take a stand is to take a stand. The churchmen who were silent when Hitler came to power were actually casting a ballot for him. They were seen as at least acquiescent and probably supportive.

Try the principle on almost any issue alive in the American churches. A young man wishes to be a conscientious dissenter. He comes and asks his pastor for support: he cannot in conscience and good faith serve in a war he finds to be immoral and unjust. If the pastor does support him, speak for him, share his conviction, or at least admire his courage, he can be accused of having taken a political stand which will compromise the Church. Dissent is, quite naturally, unpopular—otherwise it would not be dissent.

Suppose the pastor says, "I agree with you, young man. In fact, if you feel about a war as you do and then serve, you would —in classic Christian teaching—be a murderer if you kill. But while I agree with you, I cannot take your side. The position is unpopular. What is more, the law as it now stands makes no provision for exempting someone like you, and we have to support the law." Such a decision, whether publicized or not, would not be avoidance of a political position: it would be taking a political stand. It would be assent to a bad and immoral law, simply because dissent would be unpopular or strenuous.

In another instance, suppose the issue of open housing came into a community. The realtors and their allies organize to prevent its passage, on the excuse that they are only serving the clientele's interest, the vast majority of whom want to keep the communities all white. Suppose further, as is probably the case in many suburbs, that the majority of the people who vote are members of the churches. If the ministers and other leaders effectively worked to change the attitude or were able to point out that the clientele did not all feel the way the realtors said they did, the result could be important for a change in housing practices. A minister and the leadership of a church feel that present practices are not proper, not Christian: they rob people of their rights, and contribute to the impoverishment of the white community and the human problems of the ghetto. But they say that on principle they cannot undertake exposure of the issue on church property, for fear of creating dissension or because they do not believe in mixing politics and religion. To the realtors and antiopen housing forces their vote can be considered a vote for the old policy. By not taking a stand they have taken a stand.

One could continue the cases indefinitely. Politics does not allow for a vacuum. When the question is put and a test is made, silence—with the rarest of exceptions—is itself the taking of a stand. The large conservative "a-political" church bodies and congregations know this and so do the conservative business and other interests of the country—and both profit from the alliance.

None of this should be construed to mean that the churches have to involve themselves in comment on every issue which confronts city council or the United States Congress. It would be possible to nibble and nickel-and-dime away all the spiritual energy by such trivialization. Nor need the churches endorse political candidates in every kind of contest. The issue applies only to those rare and urgent "shape-up" causes in which the eyes of the nation focus on churches and clergy, who are supposed to be some sort of moral mentor. One can usually spot immediately what those issues are in any generation: they are discussed constantly off church premises but treated with silence or ginger on church premises.

To say that the churches inevitably have a political role is not to present all the ways in which it should adopt it. It is quite possible, for example, that the political sermon is an unfair and ineffective means for raising the issue. Not all ministers have competence to speak with authority on all issues. More important, the static format of the modern sermon in the face of the row upon row of pews would guarantee ineffectiveness. Late in the career of President Johnson an Episcopal clergyman addressed a number of questions about the ethics of a war to the President. The chief executive suffered in silence and no one profited from the occasion. The clergyman met with much criticism. Now, had the President risen on the spot to respond and a dialogue ensued, there would have been communication and progress. But given the current etiquette of the pew, he would have been faulted had he done so. Progress comes not when one has a privileged, raised, traditional position from which to harangue. Progress comes when Christian people encounter each other on the same level.

Similarly, it is questionable whether the constant issuing of statements on ethical positions by boards or denominations in assembly are of much promise. Those who have observed legislators in action know how short is the route from their mail pile to the waste basket, so far as formal proclamations are concerned. They know that boards of the churches are often unrepresentative and that elected assemblies equally operate under special circumstances which have little to do with the expression of the actual power positions of the masses they purportedly represent.

This is seen most clearly in the low regard held for the classic encyclicals of the modern papacy. Almost all of them have called for social change of a kind that would be uncomfortable in most nations. In recent America, they would be disquieting to warhawks and racists. Yet faithful Catholics who claim that the Pope is their guide in faith and morals either pay no attention or openly contradict his encyclical stands. When Paul Ramsey, a conservative questioner, asked "Who speaks for the Church?" he may have misstated much of the argument about church practices, but he raised a legitimate and fair question.

For all these reasons I have chosen not to concentrate on grandiose pronouncements by leaders or on refined argument by theological shapers. We shall look instead on what can go on in the gatherings where large numbers of Christians express themselves on day-to-day affairs and shall advocate a somewhat different mechanism, in which fewer purport to speak *for* the churches and more try to speak *to* them, to teach and to shape so that there will be people who actually inconvenience those who stand in the way of the good; people who actually bring in the new and the good.

With all this said, it remains difficult to locate the churches in political life. They have not been without effect. When the Civil Rights bills of 1965 were passed, Senator Richard Russell made a statement which located the churches and asked a question which put them in their place. He said that there would have been no chance that the bills would have passed, had not religious leadership involved itself. Then he went on to ask, "But where were you the last two hundred years?" His resentful question implied quite properly that the churches had done an about-face. In the past, he as a southern Presbyterian knew, they had provided ideological defense for slavery and segregation. Now they had done an about-face. Or in the past they were silent on social causes; now they were speaking out with an effect he as a legislator could not miss.

Russell pointed to an ongoing problem. What does it do to the moral case if religious leaders disagree with each other, or if they change from their own past positions? Will not this cause a lack of confidence in the other words of the Church? There seems to be no way to escape the problem in a free church in a free society, especially if one puts a premium on development and growth. More tragic would be a false or imposed uniformity among Christian groups on the one issue and, on the other, a refusal to change because a different position had been taken earlier. The question of public confidence is part of the risk the Church takes in all areas of life—it is not restricted to its political engagements. The risks can be minimized.

The Christian who cares about the Church in the city of man is willing to take the risk, however. He has confidence that all will be better off if both or all sides of an issue subject their stands to the word of God or to theological criteria and norms. Christians may properly differ on complex questions. Thus the issue of whether a war is immoral or unjust depends in part on some political commitments and evaluations one brings to the issue. But Christians believe that all will be better off if these commitments and evaluations are all brought under scrutiny in the light of ultimate moral commitments. It often comes as a surprise to Christians when they are faced with the idea that they ought to hold different views on race and destiny than their neighbors do who are not Christians. The surprise demonstrates the degree to which they regard the political order as autonomous, beyond the realm of Christian concern.

So Christians can point to some achievements in the 1960s: they had an impact on civil rights legislation; they provided leadership—however little and late—for the racial revolution; they were successful in taking stands on issues of housing, urban affairs, and agriculture in countless small communities. They had begun to move past the day when their forays were restricted to churchy and self-defensive legislation relating to parochial education and zoning changes for church buildings. Inspired by these precedents and nudged by an ever more outspoken younger clergy, Catholics and Protestants alike braced for decades of change. In what follows we shall look at some elements of a program for finding a place for the church as church in the search for a usable future in the city of man.

1. A program of understanding.

One is almost embarrassed to begin with something so banal and obvious as the suggestion that religious groups could do more to inform and shape opinion. After all the talk about the drama of revolution this certainly seems like a safe and innocuous suggestion. Yet, from another point of view, one is moved to ask whether much has been tried.

Again and again one comes to see that people can live in a society of mass higher education and efficient public media of communication and yet make decisions without reference to the world in which they live. The Church is one of the few inter-cultural voluntary agencies which can reach adults. Theoretically, it could be free from the trivializing influences of commercial interests in the media. Admittedly, the church is an establishment —but it is a counterestablishment, with interests different from its competitors. One would expect it to promote some understanding of the ecumenical world.

Not many North American Roman Catholics are aware of the social action undertaken by their Latin American brothers in the faith. Not many American Protestants have ever been informed concerning the varieties of life among Protestants "behind the Iron Curtain." The picture of missions presented in the typical parish has a nineteenth-century cast and would be embarrassing to most missionary workers now representing the churches. Do many Catholics know Camilo Torres and his record in Colombia? Have they ever wrestled with the implications of *Pacem in Terris* in their local communities? Have they ever asked the question whether living in a suburb might be a threat to faith? The agenda is endless.

These paragraphs may reveal an old liberal bias with their faith in education. The evidence is on my side: such programs would have an effect. Almost always a young person who spends so little as one summer serving in a ghetto comes back trans-formed; he reshapes his family and friends. Even a Presidential Commission, after having come into contact with the revolution-ary blacks and poor after the rioting, was able to come up with surprises. Whoever speaks of change and innovation does well to begin with education.

2. *Provide a climate for acceptance of persons in opinions in the face of disagreements.*

Once again, this seems like a modest step, hardly cosmic enough to be brought up in a book with a title like ours. And, once again, one must insist that the potential for change in this kind of activity has hardly been tapped. Many people are not open to opinion change because they have never been in an environment where options are presented them.

The religious gathering ought to be the place where the shaking issues of the day are faced in an interpersonal setting. Yet many members of such communities report that they must park their deepest questions and most passionate convictions at the door when they come into a church or any kind of Christian circle. The great issues of the day are discussed everywhere but in the churches. This is so in part because of lethargy: it never occurs to anyone to move beyond the churchy matters. More often, it seems to result from the fear that fellowship would be broken by the voicing of different opinions.

If that is the case, one must suggest that fellowship never existed in the first place. Here and there people might welcome, just for once, an escalation beyond trivial conversation about the weather and health. Whenever tried, the results are astonishing: when black and white Christian youths go on retreat and voice their real feelings; when parents and children discuss the gap across the generations; when a congregation sets out to decide whether to support a young man of principle in draft resistance—change results.

Rarely have such gatherings produced complete agreement or concord; if they did, the issues must have been shallow or presented superficially. But when people who unite in regard for each other and in common faith, change is possible. In recent years the nation has been told that white racism has to be confronted in the suburbs or northern cities; yet it seldom is. People are not going to take up such a topic on commuter trains or, in any programmatic way, at cocktail parties. Few institutions attract adults for serious purposes. The churches may be far down the scale among institutions which shape values today, but they are at least on the scale.

Out of such an exposure in such a climate a few gains would result, no matter what substantive conclusions come to light. People would move past the fear of the exposure to people with whom they disagree. They would demonstrate that Christian fellowship can meet tests when whole persons make up the gathering. And they would all see that a moral and theological word can be heard on hitherto unexplored topics.

3. Churches exist to occasion repentance and change.

Few other institutions or agencies exist to occasion profound self-knowledge and induce change. While guilt may be a small motor for positive action, the Christian concept of repentance is a joyful movement toward the new.

4. The power of the gesture.

Even where there is no consensus, men can act. Sometimes an individual will find that he cannot change an immoral law or end an unjust war. But he cannot himself be an accomplice. One may argue: can you be pure, if all the rest are impure? But he can spread his concept of the pure by defying what he sees to be wrong. He does not begin by seeing the social consequences of his act so much as the conscientious necessity for taking it. Yet others are moved.

The gesture allows for a man to take the way of the cross when society does not allow for it. He may have to be a victim. Yet his action, like that of the persecuted before him, can awaken the conscience of others. The man of the gesture is already a man of the future: he lives where he hopes others will as time passes. He may seem to be isolated, but if he acts in the context of a community, a social purpose can be implied in the gesture of the lonely.

5. The power of witness.

Gesture speaks out of community to community; witness is, in this context, gesture in the plural. It is a representation of community. Witness is superior to gesture theologically; Christians are to be members of each other. It is superior tactically, for it verges on being a political force.

An example will illustrate the difference. When the issue of support for selective conscientious objection was posed, most clergymen found no difficulty supporting the individual who found service to be contrary to his moral convictions. But such support was normally given quietly, in secret testimony and in private counsel. Yet a significant number of clergymen and religious leaders also publicized a statement they had signed in support of objectors, announcing their moral complicity and identifying with their counselees' destiny.

Criticism began at that point. A Christian minister could not fail to support the private objector in the act of moral gesture; to kill in a war which one believes to be unjust is murder, and few ministers would like to share complicity in such an act. But the private gesture leaves the system intact; a system can always afford an occasional maverick or eccentric. The witness of thousands of clerics and young men, banded together, had a larger intention. It was designed to call into question the system and the specific legislation that supported it.

Witness may take the form of such public testimony, argument, demonstration, and nonviolent noncooperation. Through such actions people become responsible to each other in their attempt to bring about change. They recognize that existing parties and organizations are part of the system and will not be likely to help effect change. Witness' approach to power lies somewhere between persuasion and aggression; it implies at least minimal organization, knowing that the defense of the existing pattern is organized and is responsive only to counterforce.

6. Work for direct political effect.

Direct political effect moves beyond witness in that it transforms the witnessing group into sustained organization. For it, denominations and parishes are not well-equipped. They have drawn people together on a variety of bases and have no real reason to assume sufficient unity on political action (or on moral issues behind political action) to speak authentically or naturally. Here interest groups, cells, units, campus organizations, will normally be more honest and efficient expressions of political intent. Politics may imply work through parties, through community organizations, or other agencies which work for change.

Political organization is the normative path in this sequence. The problem: when matters are proceeding healthily, forces like the Church are not necessary as political agents. When they are not in healthy condition, political action is often insufficient and forces like the Church have to find extraordinary and sometimes para-legal means to give new life to the society. To be effective, it would have to be part of a coalition of dissent, not for subversion as minority but to become an effective majority.

The Church might even become an agent for the building of a political society where there is none, where a system is no longer expressive of the will of the people.

7. *Being forceful without force.*

When the Church becomes "forceful," it has moved beyond gesture and witness in that it seeks immediate change and cannot wait for the long and quiet awakening of conscience, but (see #6) it also cannot count on a coalition which could form an immediate majority. The Southern Christian Leadership Conference under Martin Luther King developed this technique further than it had previously been developed in the United States. Since it insists on nonviolent means it does not set out to play God, as some of the proviolent minorities inspired by Herbert Marcuse do. Recognizing that majority conscience is hard to summon for support without direct action, this forceful means seeks to effect immediate change by conscience appeals, demonstrations, boycotts.

The nonviolent approach was pioneered by Gandhi, who built it upon love for the enemy and faith that he could become converted. In this it differs from many proconflict groups which thirst for violence, the euphemism for killing. Nonviolence wants to keep people on both sides alive so that they can have dignity, freedom, and an opportunity to make a contribution in the future.

Many have argued that nonviolence will not work on Christian and American soil because of the long historic commitment to killing on the part of Christians and Americans. There had been a long similar commitment by Hindus in India and even more by the British there; yet Gandhi became reasonably effective. Paul Goodman has written a tribute to the potential of this philosophy and tactic. "It challenges unconcern. It attacks institutions and confronts people as well. It personalizes the conflict so that habitual and mechanical responses are not easy. It diminishes strangeness. It opens possibilities for the narrow to grow and come across, instead of shutting them out. It interrupts the downward spiral of the oppressed into despair, fanaticism, and brutality. Most important, it is the only realistic strategy, for it leads to, rather than prevents, the achievement of a future community among the combatants."[66]

No one pretends that nonviolence is passive and nonaggressive. The holders of the four aces are not looking around for a new deal. They have to be stimulated and inconvenienced and conscience-pricked. Gandhi and King stimulated conflict where there had been superficial peace in order to stimulate change. The border between violence and nonviolence is very thin, as Gandhi and King both knew. Their enemies often pointed out that after they came on the scene, the situation was not so serene as before. The leaders knew this. They were working for ultimate reconciliation and peace at a less expensive price than the only other route, pure violence, would have taken.

This political nonviolence is not to be equated then with the New Testament's picture of pure passivity, of turning the other cheek. The Biblical lover of the enemy is ready to take anything, for he cannot contribute to killing and conflict. Christ's people then make the final kind of witness, sacrificial suffering. Nonviolence may also be sacrificial and certainly implies suffering, but with a positive political intent, to work on conscience and to bring about change. It remains a beautiful instrument in a less than wholly corrupt society, but is effective only when there are potential conversion and access to conscience and change. Where there are massive resistance and recalcitrance and no chance of developing an eventual political majority, nonviolence is less effective.

Daniel Callahan has said, in that instance, nonviolence is one of the moral options, however threatening: "It may not be much, and it may not be enough, but it is something. Not all ways of losing are equally worthless."[67] I would take the more positive path and say that not all ways of partially winning are equally deplorable. Being forceful without force, engaging in nonviolent political action, would be one of these ways, more congruent with Christian witness than most alternatives when a system has broken down or become repressive and politics is no longer a creative element on the scene.

8. Violence.

Once again, history's dirty secret comes to the fore. A summary may be in order. The Christian can never write an *a priori* defense of violence because violence means potentially depriving another of life, and thus violating the law of God. In this reading, killing even in self-defense is not to be justified but occurs only when an "ethic of distress" is operative. In the statements of the Sermon on the Mount, the Church's most sustained recall of Christ's teaching on such subjects, no allowance is made for defense of self or nation.

While no defense in advance or no programmed violence is tolerable, the Christian recognizes that the line between nonviolence and violence is relative and not absolute: there are more ways than one of killing, as Christ himself recognized in his diagnoses and proscription of hate. And when counteractive violence occurs, it takes its root in a violence already on the scene: the new force has not introduced but has met violence.

For all of these reasons, we place violence last, as a last resort and not as a justifiable option, even though it may necessarily be utilized in extreme situations and when all other recourse has given out. It is part of the technique of brinkmanship which the nonviolent and which all people in politics employ, though successful political agents do so with restraint. Sometimes the threat of violence prepares a climate wherein nonviolent action becomes a relief, a tolerant, welcomed, and effective instrument. Without the threat, no change would be foreseeable.

The language of violence, when this means killing, would inevitably have to be de-escalated in the Christian vocabulary. The penultimate words are conflict and separation; the ultimate words for Christians are peace and reconciliation. When people habitually resort to the threat of violence, they also threaten the permanent breakdown of community and thus defeat some of their own purposes. Nonviolent and other kinds of political action also leave scars, but not necessarily permanent wounds. Recall? We are not looking for Utopia, but for a usable future.

9

A People for the Future

"*W*ithout vision the people perish." This is a book about people, not about books or disembodied ideas. We have been concerned to see how various approaches to the future of man and society affect the actions of people. For the most part, there has been little mention about the health and state of the particular people, the members of the Christian Church. Yet if they are to take their place among other agencies of power, there must be assessment of their own condition and of their own view of the future.

Christians have shared with other children of their generation a kind of historical amnesia or even a rejection of the past. That past has seemed useless to many of them; the tradition is exhausted. They have experienced some of the sense of schism and disruption of which Nicholas Berdyaev spoke. There is little sense of continuity with the long Christian past. Conservatives and many members of the older generation in the Church are reduced to longing for the good old days, the presumed Golden Age of the immediate past. Many reformers have drawn on deeper, richer, longer traditions from the remote past to provide a measure of choice in decision in the present. And the more radical reformers have contended that little in the past can speak to today, that Christians must begin at the beginning.

If many Christians are victims of recent bad history or resentful of the tradition itself, they are also defensively related to the present and the unfolding future. Both the pervasive secularity and the bewildering religiosity of the late twentieth century pose problems to the believing community. Some have lapsed into a new determinism, to wait for the end or to mourn for the passing of old glories. Others have seized initiative and speak stridently, as if they were in control of history; they have not yet turned in their cards as "Boss of the Universe." It is difficult for them to see in what ways they are to retain the best from the past and in what ways they are to be innovators, agents of change.

An incident from my own recall will provide a model for a vision of the assertive Church in a changing world. It is an unromantic story, with no clear white and black lines of good and bad people; it contains enough ambiguity and complexity to give me confidence that it can serve as a paradigm for our kind of time.

Several years ago a professor of Missions at the Divinity School of the University of Chicago was speaking to a student-body luncheon. His theme: when graduates received their doctoral degrees, they should not all converge on the prestige schools of an affluent society. In an age when their contemporaries were seeking at least temporary careers in the Peace Corps and similar service agencies, they could find new purpose by going to teach in universities, colleges, and seminaries established in other cultures by the Christian missionaries of the past two centuries. Many of these schools were cut off or wanted to cut themselves off from sponsoring denominations in the Western world and wanted to upgrade themselves to provide leadership for the indigenous churches.

After the talk, during a discussion period, an advanced student in the field of History of Religion, where a high valuation is placed on the primitive religions, made a comment in criticism of the appeal. He averred that students should not respond. The schools should be starved out and closed down. They should not continue the Christian mission and Western churches should make no contribution to their continued health. They had been too disruptive of traditional cultures, and would continue to be an abrasive force. While everyone in the room had read Melville or Michener on the abrasion of cultures when missionaries arrived, someone pressed him for illustration to make his point perfectly clear.

He chose to do this through a parable from Latin America and by reference to the Bororo Indians. He told of a Bororo village, where the huts had been aligned with four corner pillars, which represented the corners of the cosmos. At the center, as in the classic primitive cultural symbolism, was the "holy hill," the sacral center. People were oriented to these positions and their cultural life was determined by their view of the sacral.

Then came the Jesuits.

The missionaries did what missionaries have done for centuries: they built a clinic, a school, a chapel; they served the people and made converts. Transition came. The chapel was not at the center of the village, and the old shrine came to be neglected. The pillars eventually were torn down or fell. Population grew; a new culture developed. Before long the disoriented villagers started acquiring Western habits and—in the perfect punch line—Christian diseases, like endocrine disturbances, ulcers, heart trouble, and alcoholism.

The professor of Missions responded immediately, "Be glad it was the Jesuits." He then enlarged upon his surprise endorsement of Catholic missions, for he himself was Protestant. "Do you think we who work full time with questions like that are not fully aware of the abrasion of cultures, the faults of past missionaries, and the dangers in all of life?" He went on to explain himself. He argued that students of the primitive could hope at best to keep anthropological museums intact for another ten years after the time when the missions would have reached them. But these villages were being assaulted by technological orders and by their own governments, which were eager to develop their up-country regions.

In the professor's reading, change would come anyhow. "If you want to fault the missionaries, fault them for building the clinic." Once one wants to alleviate suffering, he also contributes to health; there is a decrease of the infant mortality rate and a rise in population. If people are to live, there must be more efficient supply of food: better seed, chemical fertilizers, implements, better means of harvesting and storing. (I suppose one should insert here: with this come competitive dealerships, advertising, the Bororo equivalent of Madison Avenue, and *then* endocrine disturbances, heart trouble, and alcoholism!) "But be thankful it was the Jesuits, for they at least provided alternative order, by building the chapel." People in the face of mindless, relentless change could at least reorient themselves with a system of meaning; it is therapeutic to move from chaotic or haphazard perception of reality to an organized view. The question, therefore, could not be the isolated one: should the Jesuits have come? Rather, one would have to ask, How would the change have looked if there had been no interpretive center during the time of transition?

We now leave my colleague and the student, with due apologies for any inaccuracies or embellishments of the story. Technology had not yet reached my office, the moral equivalent of a Bororo village; I did not have a tape recorder to capture the quick exchange. Nor am I in position to appraise all details of the story; all thoughtful people have pondered the general outlines of such encounters and appraised their moral ambiguity. Instead, it is time to draw out some implications.

Picture Western culture as a Bororo village; the shrine is neglected, but still present. The pillars remain, though they are eroding. Sudden, complete, and devastating change is upon it. No one, in an age of the media revolution, escapes the dimensions of the psychic impact. What might be the role of a potent religious force at such a time?

In the Bororo picture, the Christian presence meant at least the following: the initiation of change; the exploitation of change;

the interpretation of change; and the anticipation of further change.

To initiate, inaugurate, or innovate: the responsible Christian is impelled by a cue from the future, the infatuation with the possible, the attraction of the absolute future, and the promise of Jesus Christ, to bring in the new. He does not let things remain as they are, in his own life or in society. He seeks change. He enters where he has not been before, to stimulate newness and experiment. How he does this remains an urgent question: whether he has always had a right to carry on his mission in the way he did is open to debate. No one lacks evidence of the times when he has been arrogant, presumptuous, thoughtless, too sure of his credentials as an author of the new in history. But that he must seek to relate to a coming Kingdom and to the making of all things new is not the same question as the "how."

Beyond initiation, there is exploitation. This is an ugly word, in many of its connotations. But here it represents nothing more than the taking advantage of a new situation for a better, other purpose than others had intended. It refers to the situations in which some other agency—for example, modern technology or modern political revolution—has come upon the scene to uproot the traditional culture, whether or not the Christian is present. By exploiting we mean that when everything is "up for grabs," the Christian sees to it that his presence and his option be there for possible contribution. He makes an attempt to bring purpose and order in a situation which would have been full of ruthlessness, neglect, and dehumanization.

The third strophe is: to interpret change. For some, this means that the Christian must be present with a whole systematic view of life. He must offer modern culture a fresh synthesis, a scheme into which all the random and haphazard apprehensions of the world of effects will neatly fit: the Jesuit chapel down the street from the crumbling shrine. Such an integrative or integral vision, such a synthesis may be denied people in our time. But the Christian can be of aid in providing an interpretation of life. The dictionary brings to mind the fact that to interpret means to construe reality in a particular way.

The interpretive motif does not mean that one must operate with illusions, must strait-jacket or distort reality. The Christian cannot wheel God out on stage and prove his existence; he cannot provide a philosophically satisfying answer to the problem of evil. He points to Christ crucified, who complains of godforsakenness and shouts triumph, who dies in the condition of broken existence but lives.

Finally, the Christian anticipates further change. Here the prophetic or protestant principle comes into play. He does not rest content when he has built his clinic to serve, his school to teach, his chapel to interpret reality; he subjects his own work to scrutiny and immediately begins to move on. None of this need be done with grim, humorless obsession; but the forward momentum of history does not let him reach stasis or settle for complete rest.

When the Christian Church has been healthy, it has shown forth some of the marks indicated by this parable. Today it rarely looks like an inaugurator of change. Itself a traditional institution, it has experienced the presence of new agencies of innovation, new topplers of its own pillars and shrines, new challenges to its own orientation. Inevitably the Church has often looked like an agency of the status quo in many traditional cultures. Where that is the case, the marks of impending death are present.

The Church at such a moment is in quest of a usable future. Many are writing alternative scenarios for it; there are numerous "as ifs," great probes and imaginative projections. The creation of explicit paradigms and the working out of possibilities in the light of the options is full of promise. We shall indulge in the act of playing some futures-games, in quest of a vision and for the elimination of some alternatives.

1. Triumph. The first game depends upon a scenario that developed with the rise of the modern world. When the Church was in its institutional prime, lording it over "the known inhabited world," it could take for granted its position. With the revolt of the Catholic kings, the end of divine right sovereignty, the rise of secular states, and the extension of modern consciousness, many Christian leaders reacted against defensiveness with "triumphalism," which argued that Christianity must prevail in the world, must overpower, dazzle, overwhelm, awe, and humiliate its rivals in order to keep its position in the world and impress others with the need for faith.

The Triumph-game carries with it the implicit but never-stated assumption that the faith's future depends upon the restoration of Christendom. Only when the tall towers of total Christendom rise again can there be the kind of culture on the basis of which faith becomes plausible and widespread. Since it is difficult to envision how this would come about without coercion and the restoration of legal Christian states (something which almost no one advocates or envisions), the triumphalists have become revisionists, settling for half a program.

The Triumph-game depends upon statistics, buildings, high walls, endowments, prerogatives, and prestige. Is it all worth the effort, asks a coming generation of the last triumphalists. Triumph was not the keynote of the Church's mandate nor was the overwhelming of the world inside history part of the promise. When triumphalism continues to assert itself, it depends upon pretense and illusion, "keeping up appearances," "putting on a good show," "making a false front"—all ventures which consume too many Christian energies to deserve serious consideration. When people really think through this future, few find it attractive or usable.

2. *Defeat.*   The opposite game, played by people who share many features of the triumphalist mentality, writes a (from the viewpoint of concerned Christians) pessimistic scenario. Some do it in a spirit of masochism and self-flagellation; others want to be realists. No one can understand the true situation of the Church in the world unless he has confronted the possibility.

In the Defeat-game, people see the near or the absolute disappearance of the Church. The promise that the gates of death will not prevail does not apply to the extensive sociological community which the world has seen emerge; it refers to the gathering of the faithful, which in the New Testament could number but two or three people with Christ present in their midst.

The Defeat-game has been used by some as a scare tactic: live out your years in the Church on my pattern, following my doc-

trine, my discipline—or it will disappear in the world. Fewer have
actually meant it when they issued such threats. Those who seek
the defeat of the Church in the hope that something like a phoe-
nix will rise from it seem to be romantics, unaware of how community does live in the world. The defeat and death of the
Church could issue not necessarily in the birth of a pure community; it could mean that the God of Biblical faith would be
relegated to the status of Zeus. The historian has no way of saying that cannot happen; he must wait and see. The believer who
wills the death of the Church or its defeat is impelled to think
through the implications of his willing.

3. Retrench. This is a popular, often-written scenario developed by people who have affirmed slightly more than the triumphalists or defeatists. They call for time-biding, for keeping cool,
for sitting tight in the midst of rapid change. There is no sense of
pull from the future. Instead, a safe, custodial spirit prevails. There
is return to the past, not for the sake of models and choice for the
future, but rather for the sake of the purported security of living
in the past. Like the Vatican curial party, the retrenchers feel
that God has placed a certain deposit of faith in the world, and
has made the church leaders its trustees. They are to dispense the
quantities of mystery as carefully as possible, and guard it as much
as possible.

Not only is there a passion for a doctrinal orthodoxy born, as
Eric Hoffer once said of true believers, not of mutual love of
truth but of mutual suspicion;[68] there is also a tendency to identify with the forces of conservatism in the world. The Church
takes on protective coloration by camouflaging itself along with
"the American Way of Life" or the rightist parties of Europe or
Latin American elites. Play it safe; cater to the community; defend
the old. This hardly sounds like a futures-game at all, but it is
regarded as one by its adherents and proponents.

4. Adapt. The fourth scenario is more popular among moder-
ate progressives. It asks, "Be relevant! Be plausible!" Adaptationists ask for the modernizing of the forms of the Church; the doctrines are to be streamlined—not buried but rendered palatable.
The abrasion between the Church and culture will be minimized

in the future. The basic norms of the Church are to be drawn from the culture, not from revelation or tradition. The old is presented in a new package. The best in the new media is to be appropriated for spreading the message; new forms of art and architecture and literary expression may be put to the service of the Church.

The problem with this scenario is that it assumes both that the old Church and the new world are all right, and that the main task is simply to link them up. It does not do justice to the Church's own response to the "not-yet" pull of the Kingdom and does not penetrate into the problems of the world.

5. Reform-Renew. At this point, from my own prospect, the gamesmen turn the corner and come to a more positive approach. Unlike the adaptors, those who hold to this scenario are aware of the limits of the signals the world can give and turn with hope to the tradition. They listen again to the Bible, to the creed-writers and conciliarists, the mystics, saints, poets, reformers, and prophets of the past. From what they hear, they fashion a script which outlines a church into which today's Christians can grow.

The reformers have come to prevail in the progressive centers of the Church. They have succeeded in forming the Ecumenical Movement and found a high point in Vatican Council II. They have reached into parish and seminary, research center and activist cell. Any future for the Church without a reformist-renewalist contribution would be hard to imagine, however much triumphalists, defeatists, retrenchers, or adaptationists (people who do not know who their best friends could have been) will not recognize it.

People looking back on the twentieth century will no doubt find reason for awe at the degree of reform in liturgy, Biblical studies, and the ethical patterns of the Church in an age of insecurity, when the Church hardly seemed to have a base for reform. This is not said to induce any kind of complacency, but rather to recognize with some humility and gratitude that not everything good happened twenty centuries or five centuries ago, but that a transforming spirit has been present also in a revolutionary, buffeting age.

The renewalists have often been faulted for accepting too much from the past as being normative. Much of their effort has been directed toward a reappropriation of golden moments from the Church's past: the subapostolic period, or the time when creeds were written, syntheses effected, or previous reform enacted. The renewal movements have often implied rejection of a banal or stultifying present; they have taught a new respect for the past and for endless variations on its themes.

6. *Risk.* The limits of the renewalists' scenario have begun to become evident, however, and many are moving toward more daring scripts. "Go for broke," says this imaginative projection, which focuses on the God whose essential character is his futurity and whose Christ moves toward the world with demand and promise, whose resurrected life is a sign of affirmation and a call to radical risk.

Risk implies subjecting all the teachings of the Church to radical appraisal. It does not mean jettisoning in advance the historic teachings. Nothing seems to date so fast as the modernism of a previous generation; nothing seems so fresh as a rediscovered accent which a previous generation had forgotten or dismissed. It does mean creativity and openness in relation to the teachings, to see which might speak with terrible judgment and warm mercy to a new generation.

Risk implies subjecting the forms of the Church to radical change. The reformist and renewalist parties have learned to see how difficult progress on this front is, and the party of risk will also meet with inevitable frustration in any attempts to see a transformation of church life. Most of the inherited forms are dysfunctional in the light of the intended mission of the Church. Yet despite a century of experiment, these adapted and culturally-approved forms have largely continued to preempt Christian preoccupation.

The writers of scenarios involving risk, therefore, have devoted much attention to these. Most familiar among their attempts have been those which foresee the Church as pilgrim in civilization, as a *diaspora,* a scattered, or exilic, group. Most of them see in the immediate future a great decrease in the statistical size of the Church, as people are asked to reappraise the meaning of Christian commitment and as they are robbed of some of the more secure and comforting identifications with already approved Ways of Life.

Those who would risk such identification have been hard pressed to come up with satisfying metaphors for the future. To some, the call for an exilic or diaspora church sounds like an attempt to make a virtue of necessity. A friend in the campus ministry asks for all the books he can get on small groups: "I am reading them all these days. I have to." Campus ministers deride the early postwar years when the chapels were full and when social programs filled the void in the lives of many students home from the way: mere socialization, not Christianity—so reads the dismissal. The new small groups or the idea of a Christian presence have more effect on the campus; so runs the new argument.

When religious vocations decline, there is accent on the quality of those who make new commitments; when church attendance drops, it is often pointed out that some of the better members are out doing things in the world and not attending to incense pots and that many of the worst have dropped out when they saw the Church in new ethical involvement. Some welcome decline as a ratification of their elitist impulses.

Yet there are signs that others make a necessity out of the virtue of their new picture: the mandate of Christ was not to triumph over the spirits or adapt to the world. It was to go, teach, heal, suffer, rejoice, eat and drink, bind up, exorcise, make disciples. There was little regard for a secure sociological community. So the Church should be: it is a necessity that it resume these forms and accents. That is the opposite reading.

The pilgrim metaphor seems at first to be too modest, too feminine, too passive: the Church is seen as a victim of history, unable to establish its claim anywhere. Or it may have a sectarian tendency toward lack of responsibility for culture: let the world set itself up, and then let the Church make its way rejecting almost everything. The pilgrim imagery is more Protestant than Catholic; it does little to build culture.

The positive rejoinder to such charges takes its root in the doctrine of high risk = high yield. Venturing as a pilgrim, exilic, displaced, diasporal church is an act of faith; promise is on the side of such acts. The spirit of adventure and the guard against stagnation move with such a church.

More than many who would risk like to see, the discussion of this scenario has focused on the role of church leadership. In a static, settled order it is possible to concentrate more easily on the mass of people; when the Church is pictured as in motion and in risk, the character of leadership is crucial. What is more, in a technical and specialized world it is inevitable that more questions will be asked of those who carry professional credentials and responsibilities.

The leadership of the Church in the future of the Risk-scenario is complicated by its paradoxical relationship to the culture. The ministry, for example, is expected to live off the old establishment. People pay for its services in a voluntary society, and the clergyman is dependent upon some measure of support and good will from his clientele. If he is too prophetic, he loses his audience and his base. If he is uncritical, he settles for the old. If he is mildly judgmental, he will look like a kept-prophet, a house-critic, a subsidized-protestant.

The leadership is quite naturally looking for a new location in the culture. It may "go underground," reduced in size and numbers but newly associated with secular forces, free for new coalition, less involved with keeping the ecclesiastical show going. Ministry on the campus may move from direct churchly leadership in the chapel or counseling center to the indirect form, teaching in the classroom, where the roots and extensions of our religio-secular culture are being freshly appraised. Parochial ministers seek new ways to relate their ministry to community; new kinds of chaplaincy and association with community organization provide opportunity for others.

Not a few have learned, however, that real upheaval and innovation can occur among those who serve the gathering in the more traditional places. Perhaps it was a creative moment when black ghetto leadership told Reverend Whitey to go to the middle-class suburbs and seek to transform his own people. When a bureaucrat, professor, or professional prophet is involved in controversial or compromising action in the city of man, he is playing an expectable role, with little power involved. When a nun or a parish priest or minister or, for that matter and preferably, a lay leader is similarly committed, there is a potential for a power shift as he justifies himself, reports on his action, and seeks to motivate others in his own previously unmoved power-group. It takes less courage for a cardinal to take a clear racial stand than for a priest in a backlash ethnic parish. But if the priest begins to be successful, he may actually be doing more to occasion change in the city.

The leadership of the Church in the Risk-script will be less conscious of the need to be relevant, adaptationist, or plausible and more aware of the need to be himself. If the leader claims to be representing the Lordship of Christ in the city of man, he should expect to be some sort of creative misfit. I have often wondered whether anyone was converted by the subtle evangelism or apology of the secular or worldly theology. Why did so few "outsiders" review the books of those who wanted to build bridges to or affirm the world of the outsider? While a generation set out to show how much like the world the Church could be, the secular world showed more interest in some angular, misfitting, inner-directed people who tried to show how far the world would have to go in order to respond to "hope projected backward." Pope John, Albert Schweitzer, Paul Tillich, Martin Buber, and countless other men of great and deep spirit were the subjects of much curiosity, even though they moved by some mysterious and not easily appropriated urgings.

In a dialogue with an agnostic Jew, held in the presence of collegians who were contemplating ministry, I asked him what he most looked for from Christian ministers. He was well acquainted with all the relevant reverends, the hip and swinging clerics, the secular clergy. But he said, "I wish they would try to speak of and live with their own greatest teachings. If I could believe these, I would. Since they claim to, I would like to see how different the world would look if incarnation, crucifixion, and resurrection were taken seriously." He was not appealing for a fundamentalist rephrasing or freezing of these teachings, he made clear. He wanted them spoken of in a new day with some of the power, terror, awe, and celebration that must have greeted them when first they reached into the human city.

Few are able to write in detail concerning the precise forms for the Church in the future. It is worthwhile to experiment; Stephen Rose's *The Grass Roots Church*[69] is a creative and explicit attempt at such scenario-writing. While few act on the basis of such detail, they are inspired to risk more than they have in the past. Overpreoccupation with institutional change will not be the most urgent task in an age when young people want to reject all forms of institutions, but it also cannot be avoided, for people do make up their minds about the issues of faith and nonfaith in no small measure according to the impressions they receive from the health and form of the community.

Ten years before I wrote these lines I asked for institutional risk on the basis not of anti-institutionalism or institutional nihilism but with a regard for the difficulty of starting from scratch. The suggestion that "we already possess the institutions we need to undertake the religious task" before us was picked up by some as a sign of what came to be called "morphological fundamentalism."[70] To undertake meant and means "to set about to accomplish, take in hand." It did not mean and does not mean to fulfill and to complete. In the intervening decade one heard much about "emerging viable structures of ministry." Yet little emerged that was durable or that did not harden into new forms occasioning defensive new morphological fundamentalism.

Meanwhile, those who risked brought in the new in the context of these institutions: Vatican Council II, clerical participation in racial revolution, the antiwar movement, secular-radical-death-of-God theology, and an address to the crisis of faith were born. I hope that the *formal* change will be more sudden and complete than it has been, but the record of these years shows that epochal changes in action, thought, and passion can occur before people have completely revised the forms. As before, then, one can look for an exilic or pilgrim church not making its way to Utopia but living in that world where God carves the rotten wood and rides the lame horse—now creating upheaval and innovation, and newly marked by the sign of hope.

$\mathcal{N}$otes

1   See Barton J. Bernstein (ed.), *Towards a New Past: Dissenting Essays in American History* (New York: Pantheon, 1968).

2   In *American Heritage,* XVI: 2 (February, 1965).

3   On stopping to think, see the references in G. J. Renier, *History: Its Purpose and Method* (Boston: Beacon, 1950), p. 14, footnote 1.

4   The phrase relates to the work of William Prescott in R. W. B. Lewis, *The American Adam: Innocence, Tragedy, and Tradition in the Nineteenth Century* (Chicago: University of Chicago, 1955), p. 160.

5   On the concept of the generation, see Marc Bloch, *The Historian's Craft* (New York: Knopf, 1953), p. 185.

6   A typical criticism is in Neil Middleton (ed.), *Catholics and the Left* (Springfield, Ill.: Templegate, 1967), pp. 31–37, "Culture." Richard Hoggart and Raymond Williams are two Britishers who have carried on consistent criticism of the media from the Left.

7   For examples of essays representing this point of view, see Theodore Roszak (ed.), *The Dissenting Academy* (New York: Pantheon, 1968).

8   The phrase is from a book title by Nicholas von Hoffman (Chicago: Quadrangle, 1968).

9   An account of these trends is in William Braden, *The Private Sea: LSD and the Search for God* (Chicago: Quadrangle, 1967).

10   In William Hamilton and Thomas J. J. Altizer, *Radical Theology and the Death of God* (New York: Bobbs-Merrill, 1966), pp. 17–18.

11   Emile Durkheim, *The Division of Labor in Society*, tr. by George Simpson (Glencoe, Ill.: The Free Press, 1949), p. 169.

12   These lines relate to an argument occasioned by Paul Ramsey, *Who Speaks for the Church* (Nashville: Abingdon, 1967).

13   Emphasis mine; quoted by R. W. B. Lewis, *op. cit.*, 68.

14   Bell outlines his program and accounts for others, including de Jouvenel's in "The Year 2000—The Trajectory of an Idea," *Daedalus*, Summer, 1967, pp. 639 ff. See also Herman Kahn and Anthony J. Wiener, *The Year 2000* (New York: Macmillan, 1967).

15   Robert Boguslaw, *The New Utopians: A Study of System Design and Social Change* (Englewood Cliffs, N. J.: Prentice-Hall, 1965).

16   This typically unfortunate coinage refers to "the realm of artificially created things which behave in a life-like manner." See Richard R. Landers, *Man's Place in the Dybosphere* (Englewood Cliffs, N. J.: Prentice-Hall, 1966).

17   Paul Elmen, *The Restoration of Meaning to Contemporary Life* (Garden City, N. Y.: Doubleday, 1958), p. 189.

18   Jacques Ellul, *The Technological Society* (New York: Knopf, 1964).

19   Robert Adolfs, *The Grave of God* (New York: Harper & Row, 1967), p. 44.

20   Herbert Marcuse, in Robert Paul Wolff, Barrington Moore,

Jr., and Herbert Marcuse, *A Critique of Pure Tolerance* (Boston: Beacon, 1965).

21 On *bricolage,* see Claude Lévi-Strauss, *The Savage Mind* (Chicago: University of Chicago Press, 1966), pp. 16–36.

22 "Twelve Modes of Prediction," in Julius Gould (ed.), *Penguin Survey of the Social Sciences 1965* (Baltimore: Penguin, 1965), pp. 96 ff.

23 Arthur C. Danto, *Analytical Philosophy of History* (Cambridge: Cambridge University Press, 1965), pp. 1 ff.

24 Raymond J. Nogar, *The Wisdom of Evolution* (New York: The New American Library, 1966), p. 319.

25 Nicholas Berdyaev, *The Meaning of History* (Cleveland: World, 1962), pp. 16 ff.

26 Jacob Burckhardt, *Force and Freedom* (New York: Meridian, 1955), p. 73.

27 See the essays in J. H. Plumb (ed.), *Crisis in the Humanities* (Baltimore: Penguin, 1964), especially pp. 71 ff.

28 The first American appearance of these ideas was in *Prisoner for God,* tr. by Reginald H. Fuller (New York: Macmillan, 1957), pp. 122 ff.

29 For convenient summaries, see Colin Williams, *Faith in a Secular Age* (New York: Harper & Row, 1966), and Ronald Gregor Smith, *Secular Christianity* (New York: Harper & Row, 1966).

30 I John 2:15.

31 "Towards Eliminating the Concept of Secularization," Gould, *op. cit.,* pp. 169 ff.

32 *The Temper of Our Time* (New York: Harper & Row, 1967), p. 20.

33 Gal. 4:3, 9.

34 *Op. cit.,* pp. 87 ff.

35 A book title of Gibson Winter (New York: Macmillan, 1963).

36 See note 23.

37 C. Williams, *op. cit.,* pp. 21 ff.

38 Thomas Luckmann, *The Invisible Religion* (New York:

Macmillan, 1967); David Martin, *op. cit.*, and *A Sociology of English Religion* (New York: Basic Books, 1967); Ernest Gellner, *Thought and Change* (Chicago: University of Chicago Press, 1965); J. Milton Yinger, *Sociology Looks at Religion* (New York: Macmillan, 1963); Gerhard Lenski, *The Religious Factor* (Garden City, N. Y.: Doubleday, 1961).

39   John 14:9 and 12:44 (RSV).

40   Günther Bornkamm discusses this point in *Jesus of Nazareth* (New York: Harper & Brothers, 1960), p. 56.

41   In *Theological Studies,* XXIII, No. 1 (March, 1962), pp. 1 ff.

42   "Science humaine et conditionnement de la foi," in *Dieu aujourd'hui* (Paris, 1965), pp. 140–41.

43   Paul Tillich, *On the Boundary* (New York: Scribner's, 1966), p. 75.

44   Alfred McClung Lee, *Multivalent Man* (New York: Braziller, 1966).

45   Daniel Jenkins, *Beyond Religion* (Philadelphia: Westminster, 1962), pp. 26 ff., summarizes these attacks.

46   Harvey Cox, *The Secular City* (New York: Macmillan, 1965), p. 2.

47   Walter Lippmann, *A Preface to Morals* (paperback edition; Boston: Beacon, 1960), pp. 327 f.

48   *Op. cit.,* p. 28.

49   New York: Herder and Herder, 1966, pp. 184 f.

50   Roger Garaudy, *From Anathema to Dialogue* (New York: Herder and Herder, 1966).

51   On the social character of Christian reality, see Brian Wicker, *Toward a Contemporary Christianity* (Notre Dame, Ind.: University of Notre Dame, 1967), pp. 222 ff.

52   "Hope without Faith: An Eschatological Humanism without God," in Johannes Metz, *Is God Dead?* (New York: Paulist Press, 1966), pp. 32 ff.

53   Quoted in Jürgen Moltmann, *Theology of Hope* (New York: Harper & Row, 1967), p. 16.

54 Paul Ricoeur, *History and Truth* (Evanston: Northwestern University Press, 1965), p. 94.

55 William A. Luijpen, *Phenomenology and Humanism* (Pittsburgh: Duquesne University Press, 1966), p. 138.

56 Spoken at the Christian Unity Octave, 1966.

57 Paul Tillich, *Systematic Theology,* Vol. I (Chicago: University of Chicago, 1951), p. 87.

58 Robert L. Heilbroner, *The Great Ascent: The Struggle for Economic Development in Our Time* (New York: Harper & Row, 1963), p. 179.

59 "Taches de l'éducateur politique," in *Esprit,* 7–8/1965; pp. 78 ff.

60 Hannah Arendt, *On Revolution* (New York: Viking, 1963), pp. 18 ff.

61 Paraphrased by Arendt, *op. cit.,* p. 288.

62 Thus Michael Novak, "The Absolute Future," in *Commonweal,* Jan. 13, 1967.

63 *Out of Our Past* (New York: Harper & Brothers, 1959), pp. 87 ff.

64 Ricoeur, *op. cit.,* pp. 243 ff.

65 Joseph Sittler, *The Structure of Christian Ethics* (Baton Rouge: Louisiana State University Press, 1958), p. 83.

66 "Reflections on Racism, Spite, Guild, and Violence," in *The New York Review of Books,* May 23, 1968, p. 22.

67 "Resistance and Technology," in *Commonweal,* Dec. 22, 1967, p. 381.

68 Eric Hoffer, *The True Believer* (New York: The New American Library, 1955), p. 114.

69 New York: Holt, Rinehart and Winston, 1966.

70 See the comment of Peter L. Berger, *The Noise of Solemn Assemblies* (Garden City, N. Y.: Doubleday, 1961), p. 159.

Index